from **india**

from
india

over 100 recipes to celebrate
food, family & tradition

kumar & suba
mahadevan

Thunder Bay
P·R·E·S·S

San Diego, California

This book is dedicated to my family, who are the strength and pillars of my life: my "Patti" grandmother, who lay the foundation for my culinary journey; my amma for pampering my palate; my appa for all his guidance and support; my "better half," the beautiful Suba, for encouraging me, being a part of my life and having patience, and your tireless efforts in researching for this book, traveling with me to the corners of India, and for braving all the meat and seafood prep despite being a strict vegetarian. And our sons: Abhinav and Akilesh, for sweetening our lives and for assisting us at Abhi's and Aki's.

contents

foreword

In 1994, Australia was well on the way to becoming one of the great food nations. Restauranteurs, including Gilbert Lau and Stephanie Alexander in Melbourne, and Janni Kyritsis, Tony Bilson, Neil Perry, and Tetsuya Wakuda in Sydney, were leading the charge.

I was the food critic for the *Sydney Morning Herald*, sharing the role with Helen Greenwood. The Mod Oz–French style was well established, and I made it my mission to search Sydney for great ethnic restaurants. Gilbert Lau's Flower Drum had shown us how good Cantonese cuisine can be, with stunningly good Australian produce combined with authentic Chinese techniques; Tetsuya was inventing his own modern Japanese/French hybrid cuisine to worldwide acclaim, but the other great ethnic cuisine, Indian, was a mess. I encountered fire-engine-red kebabs, cardboard-dry tandoori chicken, searingly hot vindaloos, soggy breads, and curries with boring, singular tastes. Under all the bad spicing lurked indifferent ingredients. This was an insult to a great cuisine. In London, Bombay Brasserie and The Red Fort had proven Indian cuisine had a place at the very top, so what was wrong with Australia, where Indian equaled takeaway, or something cheap and nasty?

I stumbled into Abhi's for a quick lunch on my way from a business meeting. It looked like any other suburban Indian restaurant, and my expectations were not high. It was a true revelation. The kebabs were not red, the tandoori chicken oozed with juices and flavor, tandoori lamb chops were clearly superior cuts, the curries had an incredible array of complex, fresh tastes, and the breads were perfect. This was great traditional Indian food, cooked with proper technique and passion. I was back the next night, which ended with Kumar proudly showing me his spice-grinding machine with which he made his own masalas every day.

I soon published a review, with the headline "The Search is Over." Sydney finally had a great Indian restaurant. People flocked to Abhi's. Many restaurants have such a crush of diners after a favorable review and then sink into obscurity, but Kumar welcomed the new diners, became their friends, introduced them to the complexities of Indian food, and went on to open Aki's.

Kumar at first wanted to take traditional Indian food more upmarket at Aki's, but I suggested he do something different. "Show us the new Indian cuisine, show us the regional specialities, give us dishes we've never heard of," I urged. Kumar promised to serve the same food that was eaten at the best tables in Mumbai. Having been to India with Kumar, I believe he has done better. Kumar has simply invented his own style of Indian cuisine based on classic Indian technique, but with a wonderful Aussie accent thanks to our great produce and Kumar's unending passion to be the best.

Kumar and Suba are totally dedicated to their restaurants, and I'm sure we will continue to be surprised. For them, the search is not over.

Les Luxford

vannakkam

welcome to our table

Vannakkam is a Tamil saying meaning "welcome." The people of this state, where I was born, have a belief that serving food to others is a service to mankind. Share our culture, family, traditions, and our journey around India in this book, and learn to cook the food we love most.

kumar

Our family has an astrologer we turn to for advice when we need to make important decisions. Astrology is an ancient science and we are fortunate to have a good astrologer. He helped me find my wife, Suba, and we've been married for twenty-five years. It seemed like an odd match, but he was right. My life hasn't turned out the way some expected, but I couldn't be happier. Perhaps some things are written in the stars, but we can't always see it.

I grew up in a town called Tirunelveli, in the state of Tamil Nadu, near the southern tip of India. It sits on the western side of the Thamirabarani River, 435 miles southwest of the capital, Chennai. Everyone knew our place as House Number 108. I lived there with my grandmother Meenakshi, her two sons, my dad and uncle, and their wives, my mum and aunty, and my brother, who now lives in Australia, a sister and four cousins.

Patti, a term of respect for grandmother, is the biggest influence on my cooking. My grandmother is the salt, the prime ingredient that shaped my childhood. Patti had an amazing sense of smell, which is something I inherited from her. Smell is my greatest sense. It's my driving force in the kitchen and a key part of taste. My chefs tell me I should have been a sniffer dog. Patti Meenakshi never cooked once her children married. She sat in the corner of the kitchen watching her daughters-in-law, telling them what to do, especially the order in which spices should be added, and then sniffing the air saying, "That's burnt!" or "The aroma is lost!" She was a perfectionist.

When I started doing that to my mum, Gomathi, she responded, "You're worse than my mother-in-law!"

We are vegetarians and Patti was very firm and strict about what made a good meal. It had to include four different vegetables, two types of lentils, two chutneys, pappadoms and pickles, and two rice dishes or chapatis, but all in small amounts. She preferred variety and quality to quantity. To this day, I like my meals the same way, with all the condiments, even when I get home from work at midnight and feel hungry. My wife thinks I'm a little crazy, but she understands why.

Patti would serve us when we came home from school for lunch and teach us about the right flavor combinations and how to balance a meal. She had mystery tasting and testing games, asking us if we could pick up hidden spices and ingredients. Meals were often shared with friends and neighbors and with Patti in charge it made them fun, loving, and also educational.

MY grandmother is the SALT, the prime
ingredient that shaped my childhood.

By the time I was seven, I was very curious about flavor and taste, but Mum and Dad would say to me, "Control your tongue!" They meant you won't be academic if you give importance to your tongue. Your brain will go numb from eating so much and you won't concentrate on study. That's a Brahmin philosophy. I was raised Hindu as a Brahmin, the priestly class. Brahmins are quite academic and intellectual. They're not necessarily gourmets. They like clean tastes. I've changed a lot since then, but my food is still about clean, clear flavors.

Everyone expected me to become a doctor or engineer, but I'd sneak into the kitchen while pretending to study. I was eight when Patti taught me how to make rasam, a lentil soup that's a staple in every Southern Indian meal. Many people think it's simple, but there's a lot of complexity and subtlety in that simplicity. Patti emphasized the Ayurvedic nature of food. The term comes from two Sanskrit words meaning longevity and knowledge. It's a form of alternative medicine and there are six kinds of rasam, made according to the seasons and family needs. There are different rasams for varying ailments, from pepper rasam for colds and flu to lime or tamarind rasam for a healthy heart.

Patti would say, "Food is the essence of existence." Our family keeps her recipes and habit of healthy criticism alive to this day.

I was sixteen and had just started an economics degree at Madras University when my family's fortunes fell. Dad made and sold steel utensils, but the business collapsed and owed huge debts. I lasted less than a month at college. My father couldn't support the family and we were under a lot of financial pressure when a distant friend suggested the Madras Catering College to me. I was passionate about cooking and jumped at the chance, but I struggled to convince my parents it was the right decision. I wanted to help repay Dad's debts. A full scholarship for the three-year course helped, but

it caused a lot of family tension because it wasn't seen as the right career for a Brahmin. It was a time of upheaval and bitter struggles to go against my upbringing. One relative refused to eat at the same table with me for several months. Chefs were below him and by definition, unintelligent. I was devastated, but was about to become even more of a rebel.

My training began with a big shock on my very first day. Eating meat is a sin for Brahmins, who are even wary of onions and garlic, which are considered aphrodisiacs. I puked when I had my first mouthful of meat. I ran out of the classroom and kept vomiting. I couldn't understand the flavor or texture. I tried to avoid it, but really I had no choice if I wanted to be a good cook. It took about four months before I was comfortable with it. I trained my palate and got used to the flavors by tasting sauces rather than the meat itself.

At the end of my first year, I got a summer job at the five-star Taj Mahal Palace Hotel in Bombay (now Mumbai). I was seventeen and the least experienced of all the interns, but had unlimited energy. Conscious of the money my family owed, I signed up for double and sometimes triple shifts, working eighteen consecutive days and staying with an aunt who lived 90 minutes' train ride away. As luck would have it, they put me in the butchery section under a grumpy old chef. My first job was taking the skin off chicken drumsticks. By day two I was boning them out. The cuts and bandages on my fingers reminded me to focus on getting better. I learned on the job, handling cuts of meats I'd never seen before and becoming an expert. I worked in every section under Cyrus Todiwala, a Parsi chef who now runs London's Café Spice Namasté. Between shifts, I'd work in room service to get more experience. But I had one big problem. I spoke Tamil, not Hindi, the language of Bombay. The others teased me and made up fake terms for the kitchen techniques I was learning, but I picked up enough to get by.

My fear of meat vanished and by the time I was back at college, I was bartering with my classmates to trim their meat in return for prep I didn't enjoy, like chopping onions. I graduated in 1979, aged nineteen, and was offered jobs in nearly every five-star hotel in India. I went back to the Taj on a salary of 640 rupees (about $80 per month) and was fast-tracked, graduating in half the time. By then I also understood French and Chinese flavors, as well as loving Bombay's street food, which we'd go out to eat in our time off. This was the boost I needed—the sour slap to wake up my spirit and sharpen my mind.

I'd send half my wage home to my family, but it still wasn't enough to pay my dad's debts, even when my pay doubled. My mother needed an operation and once again fate intervened. The Sheraton opened a new hotel in Basrah, Iraq, in 1981, and I went to work there. My salary jumped tenfold. The only downside was I was moving to a war zone. The Iran–Iraq war was entering its second year and we were 12 miles from the enemy border. We had front-row seats for the conflict's regular shelling.

Home was caravan-style accommodation in the nearby staff village, but we had no life beyond the hotel—a colleague who ventured out for cigarettes came home with shrapnel in his leg—and its 15-inch-thick walls meant it doubled as a bomb shelter. When the bombardments intensified, we'd move into the hotel, sometimes for days, sometimes for weeks. The longest lockdown period was nearly two months. By 1984 the situation had deteriorated further and many senior executives had left. Produce was scarce. We'd go for months without eggs or butter. My father's debts were now repaid, and I'd had enough. I returned to Bombay.

My next adventure came in the form of a newspaper article in the *Times of India*. The Tea Board of India and Air India had joined forces to open restaurants in London and Sydney to promote our nation, and they wanted chefs. London sounded ideal. I got the job, but they sent me to Australia in August 1985. I arrived in Sydney with two other chefs, on a one-way ticket, with a permanent resident's visa. The only things I knew about my new home were that the cricket was great and that women sunbathed topless. The first thing I noticed was clear blue sky and vivid colors, but within six hours of arriving, we started our first shift at Mayur, in Sydney's Martin Place. It was a three-level fine diner serving traditional Indian food and seated 100 people. It attracted celebrities including Elton John, Mick Jagger, and the King of Bahrain. Everyone loved watching us work the open tandoor, but the kitchen was much smaller than the hotels I was used to. Conditions were tough. We worked 96-hour weeks over six days for poor pay and had signed four-year contracts with a clause that said if we left, our parents had to pay a large penalty. We shared a single-bedroom city apartment with three mattresses on the floor. I knew nothing but hard work, and my goal at the time was to survive.

A year later, I wanted to settle down, so I told my father I wanted to find a traditional Indian girl to marry. Despite all my adventures, I'm proud of my culture, which is very valuable to me and very easy to lose. I'm keen to preserve it and pass it down to my children. My father put an ad in the paper asking for an "alliance." It's such a funny word, but looking back on my marriage to Suba, it now seems just right.

this was the boost i needed—the SOUR slap to wake up my spirit and sharpen my mind.

suba is my spice girl and a must spice in all my endeavors.

I knew nothing about her, but our astrologer told my parents we were a good match. We seemed like opposites—I'm loud, energetic, and full of ambition, while Suba is shy, quiet, and calm—but the astrologer looked for compatibility in the long term and like the spices used in Indian cooking, the strength of one is mitigated and enhanced by the subtlety of the other.

Suba sent me a studio photo, but she looked too serious. The first thing that attracts me in a woman is her eyes. They speak a lot of things, but I couldn't tell from this photo, so I asked for another one and she sent one of her with her young cousin. I could see her playfulness and smile. We exchanged letters, which took two weeks to arrive, and phone calls, but didn't meet until ten days before our wedding. I couldn't afford the time or money to fly to India for our engagement. Just three months passed between the "alliance" being formed and our marriage. The engagement photos arrived just as I was leaving for India. Our traditional wedding in Chennai, in July 1987, took two days, with thousands of people attending. It went on a bit too long for my liking, before our three-day honeymoon in a hill resort called Kodaikanal. Finally Suba and I had a chance to talk.

I came back to Australia for work, and my wife followed three months later with my mother. The astrologer sent my mother, saying she had to stay until Suba and I understood each other. Mum was the bridge. He told her, "You've got to control your son and be supportive to your daughter-in-law and shield her from this devil," which is me. I call a spade a spade and I'm pretty blunt, whereas Suba is the opposite.

My father-in-law said, "My daughter's a great cook," but after we were married, I discovered she didn't know how to cook. I asked him, "Why did you stick up for your daughter?" Of course Suba is a great cook now, although she's still vegetarian.

Mum stayed for twelve months until our first son was born. I used to meet Suba in the park for a date between shifts, just to see her alone. Work was tough. A friend was making three times my wage elsewhere, so I knew I was underpaid. I was forced to go back into the kitchen just a few hours after our son, Abhinav (Abhi) was born in 1988. I carried that hurt for many years, but it taught me an important lesson in how *not* to treat people.

I was desperately unhappy and wanted to leave so I told my dad, who consulted the astrologer. He said I had a brighter future ahead, but now is not the time to leave, so I stuck on. As it happened, Mayur failed after two years and suddenly I was free. I was sick of Indian food and wanted to cook anything but curries. Suba was a tower of strength. She said I should not give up my talent.

I was cooking at Sorrentino Café in Sydney's Circular Quay in late 1989 and became friends with the owner, Doug Moxon. We decided to open an Indian restaurant together. It took six months, but we found a place in North Strathfield, and in 1990, Abhi's, named after my son, opened. Doug was a partner in the business for seven years and remains a good friend.

I wanted Abhi's to be different. There were no samosas or pakoras on the menu. I wanted both authentic and contemporary flavors to showcase the regional beauty of Indian cuisine. Palak patta chaat, a street-food classic, using chickpea batter–coated spinach leaves with three chutneys and cumin-infused yogurt, was on the first menu and soon became a signature dish. Dosa, the lentil and rice pancakes from my southern birthplace, eaten with the hand, became an instant hit.

Our second son, Akilesh, was born in 1991 and during those years we struggled until Les Luxford reviewed us in the *Sydney Morning Herald* in April 1994. He said he'd found the best Indian food in Sydney. Suddenly, we were an "overnight success" and there were lines down the street. It was all hands on deck, and I called Suba in to help in the restaurant in the evenings.

I realized Suba's true strength when a trusted staff member robbed us of a large amount of money. We were young, married four years, with two small children and fighting to make ends meet. I was shattered, absolutely devastated, and I cried. Suba said something I'll remember for the rest of my life: "This person has robbed you only of money, let him not rob you of your mental strength."

After that, I woke up and it really built my confidence. Suba is so sharp and strong. She's behind all my success, the driving force and strength in all the decisions we make. Now she corrects me all the time and she's my biggest critic. She wrote the twenty-first anniversary menu for Abhi's. That's how well she understands what we do. I am so proud of her. Suba is my spice girl and a must spice in all my endeavors.

We opened Aki's on the newly restored Woolloomooloo finger wharf, the first in a row of hip waterside eateries, in November 2003. It was a very brave thing to do because Indian food is still not accepted at the fine-dining level in Australia. There are a lot of perceptions we need to correct about Indian food, and that's what I'm trying to do there. We focus on seafood. The signature dish, crab iddiappam, is a fine example of this fusion of tradition, innovation, and great local produce. It seems to be working. In 2011, Aki's was awarded a chef's hat in the *Sydney Morning Herald Good Food Guide*.

My other passions are photography, wine, and travel. I love Australian wine, and I'm very proud of the wine lists at both restaurants. I've also been researching the history and regionality of Indian cooking. Every year, we visit our homeland to discover and better understand the flavors of India. It's amazing how the same dish can change so dramatically in appearance, aroma, taste, and texture in just a few miles.

My boys are now grown and help out in the restaurants, too. To have such a happy worklife and family is the sweet balance I've been looking for. We are a very close family and we still have quite a strong relationship with our astrologer. He's close to 80 now and still tells me do this, don't do that... He even advised us when our children should be married. We trust him completely. After all, he was right about Suba and me.

to have such a happy worklife and family is the SWEET balance I've been looking for.

suba

Kumar has *kaivasnai*, a Tamil word that means "hands that give flavor." I don't come from a big foodie family. We just ate what was given to us, which was very simple. My father's only comment about food was if a dish needed less or more salt. It took me a while to understand that what Kumar says isn't meant to hurt—and he offers criticism freely and frequently. Now I tell him, "Can you please tell me the truth?" I don't want him to say something just to be nice. Even my mother asked Kumar for help to improve her cooking.

My father, Krishnamurthi, was an engineer for All India Radio and every few years, he'd be transferred, so I lived in a lot of different regions. I was born in Chennai, started school in Jodhpur, and finished it in Sangli. After a few years in Mumbai, I moved back to Chennai, graduated with a commerce degree, and took a job as an announcer at Chennai Railway Station. My father's travels meant that I spoke four state languages—Hindi, Marwadi, Tamil, Marathi—as well as English. Kumar only spoke Tamil.

I found out about my marriage accidentally, overhearing a conversation. I discovered that our horoscopes were already matched and Kumar's parents were coming to see me. Suddenly my life was taking a very different turn. Girls of my caste married doctors and lawyers, not chefs. I was twenty-one, so shy and confused, too, so I simply left everything to my parents. There was no compulsion from our parents that we had to get married. At any time we could say no, but I still felt the pressure. Our destiny was overpowering our emotions.

I was worried about how to settle in Australia, especially since I'd never left India; however, my age was an advantage and I believed I could adapt. When they sent me Kumar's photo, I wondered how tall he would be. He had sunglasses on, so I wanted another photo. I did think he had a nice smile. I didn't have any photographs of myself, so I went to a studio to have one taken and sent it to him, but he thought it looked too serious and wanted another one.

The next step was a phone call, but I'd never made an international call before. His parents had a phone at their house, so I'd go over there to talk to him. I was so nervous. Kumar is very talkative and straight away he started asking questions. I didn't know whether to speak in English or in Tamil, and I don't think I answered any of the first few questions. He asked me if I knew how to cook. I said yes. I thought he meant the basic, simple cooking I grew up with. I simply kept saying yes to anything. It was a nervous yes. There was a lot of pressure on me. I thought if I said yes, everything would be all right. The only confidence I had was that if I said yes, I'd be able to do it. But I also felt very stressed after that first call and wondered what the next one would be about.

My initial impression was Kumar was full of life and seemed so worldly. On the second call, he made a lot of suggestions, such as driving and photography courses. After a while we both began to look forward to our calls, then Kumar asked his younger brother to go see me. He turned out to be an absolute contrast to Kumar and told his elder brother, "She's too good for you, you got more than you asked for."

We had the traditional first meeting at my parents' place, just ten days before our marriage. Kumar's parents had warned me that he's very fast, very loud, and very aggressive. My heart was pounding and my hands were shaking as I tried to pour coffees. Everyone was watching, and I was the center of attention. I was so shy I didn't even look up to his face. After ten minutes Kumar said, "I want to have a word with her separately." He asked if I'd done the things he asked me to do and once again I just

kept saying yes, yes. I didn't want to do anything to break things up and I was afraid.

One thing I really like about Kumar is there's an old-fashioned side to him. We share a faith in our parents and astrologer. My comfort was that the astrologer said our marriage would work. Yet here I was marrying a chef and I didn't even know how to use a knife and fork! After the wedding, he took me to a five-star hotel for a meal, but I'd only ever eaten with my hands or a spoon.

I was shocked when I discovered he ate meat. It never occurred to me, but it's inevitable if you're a chef. I started to accept it and because he thoroughly understands and respects the background we come from, he's fine with the fact that I remain vegetarian to this day.

Compromise and understanding are keys to a successful married life. Opposite poles attract—this really made sense to us.

Our honeymoon in Kodaikanal was the first time we were alone and that's when our life together really started. The first thing he said was, "You know, I talk a lot." I thought, what am I going to answer to this? It's true, so I said, "I know, I listen a lot," and Kumar replied, "That's good enough!"

He's very adventurous and we went rowing in a small canoe on the river. I knew nothing about water, or even swimming, and suddenly I got tired and wanted to give up. Kumar said, "No, this is how life is going to be. We've got to get across, so you'd better row," and we did it together. That moment summed up how our life together would be.

I realized right from the day I got married that the drive for perfection was a key part of Kumar. He wants everything right and if he wants something done, he'll get it done now, whereas I'm slow and steady.

When I came to Australia, I was shocked and wondered how I'd manage this person—his loud voice against my soft, shy nature, his fast movements against my slow reactions, his short temper against

my cool nature; so I kept quiet and followed him. Adjusting was difficult initially, but then love started kicking in and we felt very comfortable with each other. Two months after arriving in Sydney, I had a job working in administration with the New South Wales Police. I stayed there for fifteen years and it gave me a chance to explore the city, its people and culture, and broaden my views on life.

When the restaurant review came out in 1994 Kumar said the restaurant was really busy and he wanted me to come and help him. I had no experience, but he didn't listen. He threw me in the deep end as usual, and the first thing I did was carry prawns to a table. There's a picture of God in the restaurant and at the end of service I went and prayed, asking, "What am I doing?" But then people were happy and smiling, so why would I think it was a sin? At the end of the day, I told Kumar I really enjoyed it. He brought my strength and confidence out of me. I didn't know how to do it. Kumar did. Working with Kumar has brought us even closer together. We have a common goal in the success of our restaurants.

We travel to India on a regular basis for inspiration. Kumar loves rediscovering bygone recipes from master cooks and visiting housewives who stick to the old traditional style of cooking. He then weaves it into the food at Abhi's and Aki's.

Kumar asked me to design the twenty-first anniversary menu for Abhi's. Can you imagine it, when I'm still a vegetarian? It was such a success. This is how he brings out my strengths. I have become an integral part of his life, his business, and everything around him. Kumar and I are now so dependent on each other, and our children have seen the success of our lives and how we balance each other. We have a wonderful, close family and we are so proud of our children. It's amazing to see what we've achieved from an arranged marriage. Even today, when we go to see our astrologer he recalls how we met and says, "See, I told you."

salt

SALT IS A PRIME INGREDIENT IN SHAPING LIVES.
Without salt there is no flavor. It is the mother of all ingredients: that's the first lesson Patti, my grandmother Meenakshi, taught me. She only had to smell a curry to tell if it was seasoned properly and, thankfully, that skill passed on to me. Understanding its importance is the key to good food. My hand still shakes when I add salt. It's the one and only sensitive ingredient that makes or breaks a meal. My grandma was the salt of my childhood. She was a walking, talking recipe book with strict commands to be followed. She has always been the inspiration for my cooking, and she fed my hunger for knowledge well.

To get the best result, add salt during cooking, rather than sprinkling it on food at a later stage, but always be careful because if you add too much, the excess cannot be removed.

Natural salt is considered the prime spice in Ayurvedic cooking, as it stimulates digestion and of course is an essential part of life. There's a special volcanic salt from India called kala namak, or sanchal, that is believed to have medicinal qualities. It is also known as black salt, but when ground it's more pinky-gray in color. Kala namak has a slight bitterness and, most distinctively, a pungent sulfurous (rotten egg) smell, and it is an essential part of chaat masala (a spice mix used in chaat).

Always use good-quality salt flakes for cooking, even though they are a little more expensive, instead of table salt, which has a number of additives, including anti-caking agents. Maldon sea salt from England and Australian Murray River pink salt are two of my favorites for cooking.

When you're choosing what salt to use, put a little on the tip of your tongue and taste its strength. This sounds contradictory, but you don't want it to be too salty. A good salt has quite complex flavors and even a slight sweetness.

Sea salt acts as a balance between sweetness and acidity. It reduces sourness and increases sweetness, which is why it's also important in desserts.

A curry without salt is considered inauspicious in Hindu culture. Its importance is such that after someone dies, a feast is prepared after ten days without using salt to cook, so that the soul leaves its earthly desires and finds peace.

All these things I learned at the elbow of my grandma. I hope to keep her memory alive and pass on her wisdom in the following recipes, which are an extension of our family meals.

grandma's dal

braised lentils

My grandma Meenakshi insisted that this dal be cooked every other day. The "moong" was her favorite dal, being easy to digest. She preferred her dal with a bit of extra asafetida. Meenakshi was very particular about her diet; she never even allowed onion or garlic to enter her kitchen.

3½ oz (100 g) moong dal
(green gram) (see glossary)

3½ oz (100 g) toor dal
(yellow lentils) (see glossary)

1 teaspoon ground turmeric

6 small green chilies,
halved lengthwise

⅓ cup (2¾ oz/80 g) ghee
(see glossary)

1 teaspoon cumin seeds

1 tablespoon finely grated ginger

2 tomatoes, sliced

½ teaspoon asafetida
(see glossary)

roughly chopped cilantro
(coriander), to garnish

SERVES 4 AS PART OF A SHARED MEAL

Wash and rinse the moong dal and toor dal and put in a large saucepan. Add sufficient water to cover the dal by about ½ inch (1 cm). Add the turmeric and chilies and bring to a boil, then simmer uncovered for 35 minutes or until the dal has completely broken down, adding a little more water if it looks dry.

Meanwhile, heat the ghee in a frying pan over medium heat. Once the ghee is hot, add the cumin seeds and cook for 30 seconds. Add the ginger and cook for 2 minutes. Add the tomato and asafetida and cook for 1 minute.

Add to the dal and cook for another 5 minutes. Season with salt and serve garnished with cilantro.

avial

vegetables in yogurt curry

This is one of the very early recipes my mum taught me. It is a very simple and easy mix of vegetables with a very clean taste. The secret is to cook all of the vegetables at different stages to preserve their crunchiness. This is predominantly cooked with root vegetables. In Kerala they add peeled jackfruit seeds. If the timing is not right, it can end up as a vegetable mash.

½ cup (2½ oz/70 g) grated coconut (see glossary)

3 small green chilies, roughly chopped

½ teaspoon cumin seeds

⅓ cup (3¼ oz/95 g) plain thick yogurt, beaten

1 potato, cut into finger-sized batons

1 sweet potato (about 14 oz/400 g), cut into finger-sized batons

1 carrot, cut into finger-sized batons

3 drumsticks (see glossary), cut into 2-inch (5-cm) pieces

½ taro or white sweet potato (yam) (about 7 oz/200 g), cut into finger-sized batons

1 green banana, cut into finger-sized batons

1 small eggplant, cut into finger-sized batons

10 green beans, halved

2 tablespoons vegetable or sunflower oil

10 curry leaves

1 tablespoon coconut oil (see glossary) (see tip)

SERVES 4–6 AS PART OF A SHARED MEAL

Put the grated coconut, green chilies, and cumin seeds in a small spice grinder with 2 tablespoons of water and grind to a smooth paste. This step is very important as it provides the texture of the finished dish. Transfer to a bowl and stir the beaten yogurt into this paste.

The vegetables need to be cooked until they are just tender and soft to the bite, but not mushy, and in just enough water to cover them. Put the potato, sweet potato, carrot, and drumsticks into a heavy-based saucepan over medium–high heat and pour over enough boiling water to just cover the vegetables. Season with salt.

After 2 minutes, add the taro, banana, and eggplant, cook for 6 minutes, then add the beans and cook for 2 minutes.

When the vegetables are almost done, add the coconut paste and cook over low heat for 5–7 minutes—the yogurt tends to split, hence the need for the heat to be low, and the coconut acts as a binding agent to prevent the yogurt from curdling.

While the vegetables are cooking, heat the vegetable oil in a small saucepan over high heat, add the curry leaves, and fry for about 20 seconds. Drain on a paper towel.

To finish the dish, pour over the cold coconut oil and scatter over the fried curry leaves.

tip: If cold coconut oil is too pungent for your taste, heat the oil before pouring it over the dish.

kaali dal

black lentils

This dish is found all over India. In the north, it is called "maa ki dal" and is made with the starchy and wholesome urad dal (black lentils), but in the south it is made with toor dal (yellow lentils), which have a very low starch content. This is due to the different climates; North India gets much colder so the food reflects the need for a heavier and richer diet, and spices such as cloves, cardamom, cinnamon, ginger, black pepper, and nutmeg are used in cooking to keep the body warm, whereas in the hotter south, spices such as chili and garlic are consumed in high amounts to help the body sweat and keep it cool.

1⅓ cups (10½ oz/300 g) urad dal (black lentils) (see glossary), soaked overnight in 8½ cups (70 fl oz/2 liters) water

½ cup (3½ oz/100 g) dried red kidney beans, soaked overnight (see tip)

9 oz (250 g) tomatoes, roughly chopped, or 6 oz (170 g) tomato paste (concentrated purée)

3½ oz (100 g) butter, chopped

1 tablespoon finely grated ginger

1 tablespoon crushed garlic

1 tablespoon vegetable or sunflower oil

1 teaspoon cumin seeds

1 red onion, thinly sliced

1 teaspoon red chili powder

halved cherry tomatoes, half-and-half cream (18% fat), finely shredded ginger, finely chopped cilantro (coriander), and softened butter, to garnish (optional)

SERVES 4 AS PART OF A SHARED MEAL

You will need to begin this recipe a day ahead.

Drain and rinse the soaked dal and kidney beans, put in a large heavy-based saucepan over medium heat, and cover with about 1½ inches (4 cm) of water. As soon as it comes to a boil, reduce the heat as low as possible and cook for about 2 hours, or until the lentils and beans are tender, adding a little more water if it looks dry.

When the lentils are cooked, add the tomato, butter, ginger, and garlic and cook for 20 minutes. The secret to a good dal is cooking over low heat for a long period.

Heat the oil in a small frying pan over medium heat, add the cumin seeds, and when they turn semi-brown, add the onion and chili powder and cook, stirring regularly, for 8 minutes. This is the tempering. (See glossary for an explanation of tempering.)

When the dal is cooked, add the hot tempering, season with salt, mix gently to combine, and cook for 5 minutes. The color should be dark brown.

Ladle into bowls, add a cherry tomato half to each bowl, drizzle with a little cream, and scatter over some ginger and cilantro. For extra richness, add a small knob of butter to each bowl.

Tip: Let the lentils soak overnight to save on preparation time. It's important to use dried—not canned—kidney beans, as canned beans do not give the desired starchy texture to the dish.

rasam

tomato, pepper & tamarind soup

There is an old Indian saying, "education begins at home," and this was the very first dish I learned from my grandma when I was eight years old. It is one of the most simple dishes to make, but as with most simple dishes, the flavors must be balanced well, and timing is key. The secret is to cook it for the right amount of time and keep the flavors lingering on the tongue. Rasam is an everyday dish eaten with white rice, accompanied by other vegetables or meat. It is cooked in two stages. The first stage is with the tamarind and tomato where everything is cooked to a boiling point to make a concentrated mix. The second stage is when the cooked dal is added with water, but not allowed to boil—it should only simmer. The finished dish is a thin broth.

⅓ cup (2½ oz/70 g) toor dal (yellow lentils) (see glossary)

¼ teaspoon ground turmeric

1 teaspoon vegetable oil

½ teaspoon black mustard seeds

1 teaspoon cumin seeds

¼ teaspoon asafetida (see glossary)

3 garlic cloves, crushed

1½ tablespoons rasam powder (see page 215)

3 tablespoons tamarind pulp (see glossary)

2 ripe tomatoes, chopped

1 bunch cilantro (coriander), leaves finely chopped and stalks tied together with string

juice of 1 lime

1 teaspoon ghee (see glossary)

1–2 dried red chilies

10 curry leaves

SERVES 6 AS PART OF A SHARED MEAL

Put the dal in a heavy-based saucepan with 6⅓ cups (52 fl oz/ 1.5 liters) of water and the turmeric. Bring to a boil, then simmer for 30–40 minutes, or until soft. (Indian housewives generally cook this dal in a pressure cooker.) Set aside in the cooking water, do not drain.

Heat the oil in a heavy-based saucepan, add ¼ teaspoon of the mustard seeds and let them crackle. Then add ½ teaspoon of the cumin seeds and all of the asafetida and lightly brown the cumin, stirring regularly. Add the garlic and stir for 1 minute. Add 3 cups (26 fl oz/750 ml) of water, the rasam powder, tamarind pulp, tomato, and cilantro stalks, then bring to a boil and cook for 15 minutes. This will infuse all of the flavors together. Season with salt.

Once boiled, add the dal and the cooking water and simmer for 5 minutes—do not allow it to boil. Remove the cilantro stalks and stir in the cilantro leaves and lime juice. Remove from the heat.

To make the tempering (see glossary for an explanation of tempering), heat the ghee in a small frying pan over medium high heat, add the dried chilies and the remaining ¼ teaspoon mustard seeds, and let them crackle. Add the remaining ½ teaspoon cumin seeds and let them brown. Add the curry leaves, then stir the mixture through the cooked rasam. Immediately cover with a lid and leave for 5 minutes. This is important as the tempering will seep through the rasam to flavor it. Check the seasoning, adding some black pepper to taste. Ladle into bowls to serve.

potato karakari

spicy fried potato

This dish is an essential accompaniment to a Tamil meal, enjoyed by people from all walks of life. My son Akilesh is very fond of it. This has always been the case except for one occasion when he was about ten years old. He wanted to help me in the kitchen, so I had him peel a bag of potatoes for an Abhi's anniversary dinner in which we were serving the karakari. I think the sheer quantity of potatoes he had to peel turned him off karakari for a while… Well, at least on that occasion he did not eat any! I prefer to use kipflers, which don't need peeling—just give them a good scrub.

1 lb 12 oz (800 g) kipfler potatoes, scrubbed well and quartered lengthwise

1½ teaspoons ground turmeric

3 tablespoons vegetable or sunflower oil

¼ teaspoon black mustard seeds

1 teaspoon split urad dal (split black lentils/black gram) (see glossary)

1 teaspoon split chana dal (see glossary)

2 dried red chilies, sliced with seeds removed

⅛ teaspoon asafetida (see glossary)

2 onions, thinly sliced

2 teaspoons sweet paprika

2 teaspoons coriander seeds, crushed

10 curry leaves

SERVES 6 AS PART OF A SHARED MEAL

Put the potatoes in a saucepan of water with ½ teaspoon of the turmeric, bring to a boil, then cook for 10–15 minutes or until just tender. Drain and cool.

Heat the oil in a wok over medium heat, add the mustard seeds and let them crackle for about 20 seconds. Add the urad and chana dal and fry until golden brown. Add the chili and asafetida and cook for 1 minute.

Add the onion and cook over low heat until softened—do not brown.

Add the cooked potato, paprika, coriander seeds, remaining turmeric, and 3 tablespoons of water and cook, covered, over low heat for 5 minutes—the water assists in the spices coating the potatoes. Check the seasoning, then stir in the curry leaves and serve.

vazhakai thoran

green banana & coconut

*There is an interesting saying in Tamil, "vazai pol vazhu"—live like a banana tree.
The nature of the banana tree is always giving and sharing. Every part of the tree is used in some
form or other. Fiber from the banana plant is used as thread to weave garlands. Banana leaves
are used as disposable plates in Southern India because when hot food is served on them
the vitamins and minerals in the leaves are released—one has to experience eating on a banana leaf
to know how it enhances the flavor of a dish. The banana stem and its flowers are also
used in dishes that are eaten to remove kidney stones.*

*The banana tree is a symbol of fertility—even before a plant dies a new shoot emerges. Tamil
Brahmins have a great affinity for the banana plant, and raw banana features in almost all the major
occasions in a Tamil Brahmin household: birth, mourning, and festivities, including New Year. The
recipe below is a variation on the standard, as a strict Brahmin would not use onion or garlic.*

6 green bananas

3 tablespoons coconut oil

¼ teaspoon black mustard seeds

**1 teaspoon split urad dal
(black lentils/black gram)
(see glossary)**

**1 teaspoon split chana dal
(see glossary)**

6 garlic cloves, crushed

**2 dried red chilies, thinly sliced
with seeds removed**

¼ teaspoon ground turmeric

**⅛ teaspoon asafetida
(see glossary)**

**4 French shallots (eschalots),
thinly sliced**

**⅓ cup (1½ oz/40 g) grated coconut
or ⅓ cup (1 oz/30 g) shredded
coconut (see glossary)**

10 curry leaves

SERVES 4–6 AS PART OF A SHARED MEAL

Peel the bananas and slice into bite-sized pieces.

Heat the oil in a wok over medium heat. Add the mustard
seeds and let them crackle for about 20 seconds. Add the urad
and chana dal and fry for 3–4 minutes or until golden brown. Add
the garlic, red chili, turmeric, and asafetida and cook for 1 minute.
Add the shallot and cook until softened—do not brown. Add
the raw banana and cook, covered, for 5 minutes.

Finally, stir in the coconut and curry leaves, check the
seasoning, and serve.

vellai porrial

cauliflower & coconut

In Tamil "vellai" means white. This dish is as appealing visually as it is delicious to eat. The white cauliflower and beans with freshly grated coconut are beautifully balanced with the curry leaves, both for color and flavor, and are complemented by the sweetness of the shallot. The heat of the green and red chilies completes this fabulous dish.

1 lb 5 oz (600 g) cauliflower florets

3½ oz (100 g) double-peeled fava (broad) beans

3 tablespoons gingili (unscented sesame oil) (see glossary)

¼ teaspoon black mustard seeds

⅛ teaspoon asafetida (see glossary)

1 teaspoon split urad dal (black lentils/black gram) (see glossary)

1 teaspoon split chana dal (see glossary)

2 dried red chilies, halved lengthwise with seeds removed

2 green chilies, finely shredded with seeds removed

4 French shallots (eschalots), thinly sliced

⅓ cup (1½ oz/40 g) grated coconut or ⅓ cup (1 oz/30 g) shredded coconut (see glossary)

fried curry leaves, to garnish

SERVES 4 AS PART OF A SHARED MEAL

Cook the cauliflower in 4 cups (35 fl oz/1 liter) of salted boiling water for 5–7 minutes. Remove with a slotted spoon and set aside to cool.

Allow the water to come back to a boil, then add the fava beans and cook for 3–4 minutes. Drain and set aside.

Heat the gingili in a wok over medium heat, add the mustard seeds and asafetida, and let the mustard seeds crackle for about 20 seconds. Add the urad and chana dal and fry until golden brown. Add the red and green chilies and cook for 1 minute.

Add the shallot and sweat for 4–5 minutes or until softened—do not brown.

Add the cauliflower and fava beans and cook, covered, for 5 minutes to allow the spices to infuse the vegetables.

Finally, stir in the coconut, check the seasoning, and garnish with the fried curry leaves.

amma's dosa

spiced rice pancake

A dish originating with my grandma, fed to me by my mother as a child, and still fed to me by my wife. The tradition continues! I hope to train my future daughters-in-law to make it as well. (Mastery of this dish is a prerequisite for my sons' marriage, too!) It is a simple preparation that can be conjured up in minutes, and a fuss-free snack for the evening "tiffin."

½ cup (3¼ oz/95 g) fine semolina

3 tablespoons rice flour

3 tablespoons all-purpose flour

3 tablespoons buttermilk

ghee, for cooking (see glossary)

store-bought lime pickle, to serve

tomato chili chutney
(see page 108), to serve (optional)

TEMPERING

1 tablespoon gingili (unscented
sesame oil) (see glossary)

½ teaspoon black mustard seeds

1 teaspoon cumin seeds

¼ teaspoon chili flakes

2 small green chilies, chopped

⅛ teaspoon asafetida
(see glossary)

10 curry leaves, finely shredded

MAKES ABOUT 15

Combine the semolina, rice flour, and all-purpose flour in a large bowl with the buttermilk and 1¾ cups (15¼ fl oz/435 ml) of water and stir to combine until smooth. Set aside.

To make the tempering, heat the gingili in a small frying pan over medium–high heat, add the mustard seeds and let them crackle for 20 seconds. Add the cumin, chili flakes, green chili, and asafetida and cook for less than 1 minute. Remove from the heat and add the curry leaves. Stir the tempering into the semolina batter.

Heat a little ghee in an omelet or similar-sized frying pan over medium–high heat. Whisk the batter to combine again, then put 2 tablespoons of batter into the pan and swirl the mixture around to make a very thin pancake about 5 inches (12.5 cm) in diameter. Cook for 1 minute, then carefully flip over and cook for 30 seconds. Transfer to a plate while you make the remaining dosa, stirring the batter each time before adding it to the pan.

Serve immediately with the lime pickle and chutney.

Tip: This is an unfermented dosa batter and is not supposed to be a crispy dosa. The mixture should be more like a crepe batter.

Most Indian meals are cooked then tempered with either black mustard seeds, cumin seeds, urad dal (black lentils/black gram), and/or chilies in gingili or ghee. The critical part of tempering is not to burn or overcook the tempering and to retain the flavor and color of each ingredient. This is then added to the dish at the finishing stage and usually covered immediately so the flavors can infuse the dish.

dal & spinach massial

lentil & spinach curry

This is a healthy dish with high iron and protein content from the spinach and lentils. "Massial" denotes a dish that is a near mashed consistency, but not a purée. I have childhood memories of mashing the preparation for my mum in the kitchen with a wooden mallet. This dish was traditionally cooked in a black stone pot (makkal chatty).

3 tablespoons toor dal (yellow lentils), rinsed (see glossary)

2 tablespoons (1 fl oz/30 ml) vegetable or sunflower oil

½ teaspoon black mustard seeds

¼ teaspoon asafetida (see glossary)

2 dried red chilies

2 bunches spinach, chopped

10 curry leaves

2 teaspoons finely grated ginger

½ teaspoon crushed garlic

3 small green chilies

1 tomato, diced

SERVES 4 AS PART OF A SHARED MEAL

Put the dal in a large heavy-based saucepan, cover with about 1½ inches (4 cm) of water and bring to a boil over medium heat. As soon as it comes to a boil, reduce the heat to as low as possible and cook, covered, for 45 minutes or until tender, adding a little more water if it looks dry. Set aside.

Heat the oil in a large wok—this is necessary as the chopped spinach is fairly voluminous, but it will shrink on cooking—over medium–high heat, add the mustard seeds and let them crackle for about 20 seconds. Add the asafetida and the dried chilies and cook for about 2 minutes or until the chilies are lightly browned.

Add the remaining ingredients (except the dal), season with salt, and cook, covered, over medium heat until the spinach is cooked—do not add any water as the spinach will wilt and release enough water. Once the spinach is cooked, stir in the cooked dal and serve hot.

tirunelveli varutha kozhi

aromatic chicken curry

My hometown of Tirunelveli, in the southernmost part of India, inspired this recipe. Tirunelveli is located in a region formerly known as Nanjilnadu, ranging from Madurai to Kanyakumari, and the main spices used there are coriander seeds and ginger. This dish is finished off with crushed coriander seeds and cumin, which add a unique freshness to the curry. It is light, yet aromatic.

1 lb 12 oz (800 g) skinless, boneless chicken thigh fillets, diced

½ teaspoon ground turmeric

1 teaspoon cumin seeds

½ cup (3½ fl oz/100 ml) vegetable or sunflower oil

½ teaspoon fennel seeds

4 dried red chilies

2-inch (5-cm) piece of cassia bark (see glossary)

6 green cardamom pods

1 dried bay leaf

6 garlic cloves, sliced

1 large onion, sliced

1½ teaspoons finely grated ginger

2 tomatoes, chopped

10 curry leaves

1 tablespoon coriander seeds, crushed

½ teaspoon South Indian garam masala (see page 125)

½ bunch cilantro (coriander), leaves chopped

SERVES 6–8 AS PART OF A SHARED MEAL

Rub the chicken with the turmeric and set aside.

Meanwhile, heat a small frying pan over high heat and dry-fry the cumin seeds for about 1 minute, shaking the pan regularly. Finely crush the seeds using a mortar and pestle.

Heat ⅓ cup (2½ fl oz/80 ml) of the oil in a large heavy-based frying pan over medium–high heat, add the fennel seeds, dried chilies, cassia bark, cardamom, bay leaf, and garlic, and cook for 1 minute.

Add the onion and cook for 6–8 minutes or until browned.

Add the ginger and chicken and stir to coat the chicken. Cook for about 5 minutes. Add the tomato and cook for about 10 minutes or until the chicken is nearly cooked through.

Meanwhile, heat the remaining oil in a small frying pan over medium–high heat, add the curry leaves, and fry for about 30 seconds. Drain on a paper towel.

Add the crushed cumin seeds, crushed coriander seeds, garam masala, curry leaves, and chopped cilantro leaves to the chicken mixture and stir to combine. Season with salt and serve.

flathead pakoras

fish fritters

juice of 1 lime

½ teaspoon ground turmeric

½ teaspoon ground cumin

2 teaspoons finely grated ginger

4 garlic cloves, crushed

1 lb 12 oz (800 g) flathead fillets,
each cut into 3 pieces

½ cup (2¼ oz/60 g) chickpea
flour (besan)

3 tablespoons rice flour

2 teaspoons coriander seeds,
finely crushed

½ teaspoon red chili powder

vegetable or sunflower oil,
for deep-frying

¼ pomegranate, seeds removed

fennel fronds, to garnish (optional)

green chutney (see page 210),
to serve

SERVES 4 AS PART OF A SHARED MEAL

Combine the lime juice, turmeric, cumin, ginger, and garlic, rub all over the fish, and set aside for 20 minutes.

Meanwhile, combine the chickpea and rice flours with the crushed coriander seeds and chili powder in a flat container. Roll the fish in the spiced flour mixture.

Fill a wok or heavy-based saucepan one-third full with oil and heat to 355°F (180°C) or until a cube of bread turns golden brown in 15 seconds. Deep-fry the fish for 4–5 minutes or until golden brown. Remove with a slotted spoon and drain on a paper towel.

Serve garnished with the pomegranate seeds and fennel fronds, and accompanied by the green chutney.

jackfruit payasam

rice pudding

This was my grandma's favorite dessert. The original dish strictly uses fresh jackfruit, but we can make our life much, much easier using the canned version. Fresh jackfruit is messy as it secretes a resin that sticks like super glue, and handling it requires a lot of technique. My gran's trick was to apply coconut oil to her hands before touching the jackfruit. The seed of the jackfruit is also a popular snack, consumed like chestnuts.

1½ oz (40 g) basmati rice

2 teaspoons ghee (see glossary)

2 teaspoons unsalted cashew nuts, roughly chopped

5 saffron threads

3 teaspoons rosewater

4 cups (35 fl oz/1 liter) milk

4 green cardamom pods, crushed

½ cup (3½ oz /100 g) granulated sugar

1¾ oz (50 g) canned jackfruit, finely chopped

sultanas (golden raisins), to garnish

SERVES 6 AS A DESSERT

Soak the rice in cold water for 30 minutes, then drain.

Heat the ghee in a small saucepan over medium–high heat and fry the cashew nuts for about 1 minute, shaking the pan regularly.

Soak the saffron threads in the rosewater to make a saffron water. Set aside.

Put the milk and cardamom pods in a heavy-based saucepan over low heat and simmer, uncovered, for about 20 minutes. Add the rice and cook, uncovered, for 30 minutes or until the rice is soft.

Add the sugar and jackfruit and cook for 10–15 minutes.

Once it has thickened slightly, add the saffron water, remove from the heat, and cool slightly. It is supposed to be liquidy.

Divide among individual glasses or serving dishes and serve warm or cold garnished with the fried cashew nuts and sultanas.

Tip: Be patient and cook over low heat.

beetroot halwa

sweet beet pudding

Traditionally halwa is eaten in Northern India during winter, where it is made using the red carrots that the region is famous for, while in Southern India, they eat a version with beets all year round.

1 lb 2 oz (500 g) beets (beetroot), washed and grated

2 cups (17 fl oz/500 ml) milk

⅔ cup (4½ oz/125 g) granulated sugar

1 ¾ cup (1.8 oz/50 g) ghee (see glossary)

½ teaspoon ground cardamom

1 tablespoon raisins, lightly crushed using a mortar and pestle

2 tablespoons pistachio nuts, roughly chopped

strawberry coulis (see page 162), edible silver leaf, rose petal ice cream, and edible flowers, to serve (optional)

SERVES 4 AS A DESSERT

Put the beets in a saucepan with the milk and ½ cup (4 fl oz/ 125 ml) of water, and cook over low heat for 20 minutes or until the beets soften and most of the liquid has been absorbed.

Add the sugar, mix well, and cook for about 30 minutes or until the sugar has dissolved and all the milk has been absorbed.

Add 1 oz (30 g) of the ghee, the cardamom, and the raisins, mix well and simmer for 2–3 minutes. Remove from the heat and set aside.

Heat the remaining ghee in a small frying pan over medium heat and fry the pistachio nuts until lightly golden.

Serve the halwa hot, cold, or at room temperature in a bowl, or form into small quenelles (oval mounds). Drizzle with the strawberry coulis, garnish with silver leaf, and serve with rose petal ice cream, the fried nuts, and edible flowers if desired.

Tip: Make sure that all the beets have been cooked and there is very little water left before adding the sugar.

bitter

BITTERNESS IS NECESSARY TO BALANCE not only flavor but the struggles and realities of life. This was a lesson I learned early when I decided to become a chef and not a doctor as my parents had hoped. That was a big shock to my parents, despite me showing so much interest in cooking with my grandma. Truth is always bitter. Being raised a strict Brahmin, in which the consumption of meat or seafood is a sin, my family was completely against my chosen path of study and believed I was disrespecting my culture and traditions. It was an immense struggle to make them understand my new path of study, but my decision to become a chef was fueled with the good intention to feed people beautiful food.

From a young age, my parents taught me a saying: "Annadhatha Sukhibhava," which means, "God bless the provider of food." It is a way to express gratitude to one who provides or serves food, and using this line of reasoning that serving food is as sacred as being a devout Brahmin, my parents finally relinquished. Looking back, this clash with my parents was necessary to balance out all the good fortune to come…

Bitterness is one of the six rasas, or flavors, alongside salty, astringent, sour, pungent, and sweet, which form the basis for every meal. Indians believe that bitterness is necessary in life to balance the system. Bitter foods often have a high medicinal value, while bitter vegetables and spices can enhance the other flavors in a dish.

Spices such as turmeric, cumin, and fenugreek also have bitter characteristics. While cumin seeds are slightly bitter, they add a sweet aroma to dishes. Ground turmeric is highly regarded for stomach and liver ailments, as well as treating cuts or wounds, while anyone with a sore throat is advised to drink milk with turmeric. Turmeric is also an excellent preservative, which is why it's used extensively in Indian pickles.

Fenugreek is the most interestingly and distinctively bitter spice. Its medicinal qualities have been recognized since ancient times. Among its many attributes, the one people will appreciate most is its ability to reduce flatulence. The young leaves, called methi, can be used in salads. Most importantly, fenugreek is a valuable base note in curries. It's one of those essential scents that help you recognize Indian food.

And so it is in life too. Without the bitter struggles of my early years, I would not have recognized that being a chef was exactly what I was supposed to be.

karela masala

bitter melon curry

*Bitter melon, known as **karela** in India, is a climbing vine with bitter leaves and green fruit. A key part of Indian cooking, it's used to cut the fattiness in food as well as providing a contrast to richer flavors. It has Ayurvedic qualities that Indians believe are beneficial in dealing with diabetes and many infectious diseases, as well as having a positive effect on the metabolism. Every state has its own bitter melon recipe; this dish is from North India. The baby bitter melons are split then salted to remove some of the bitterness, then stuffed with spices and slowly roasted with ginger. This is probably our family's favorite dish. It is an excellent blend of flavors and encompasses the five tastes: bitter from the bitter melon itself, sour from the dry mango powder "amchur," spice from the red chili and turmeric, sweet from the jaggery, and salt for balance. The bitter melon is treated properly prior to cooking to cut down its inherent bitterness. The salt, amchur, and lime juice work to reduce the bitterness of the melon.*

1 lb 5 oz (600 g) bitter melon

1 teaspoon ground turmeric

juice of 1 lime

vegetable or sunflower oil, for cooking

2 red onions, thinly sliced

½ cup (2¼ oz/60 g) chickpea flour (besan)

1 teaspoon cumin seeds

¼ teaspoon asafetida (see glossary)

½ teaspoon red chili powder

4 small green chilies, chopped

2 teaspoons grated palm sugar (jaggery) or soft brown sugar

¼ teaspoon amchur (dry mango powder) (see glossary)

cilantro (coriander) leaves, to garnish

SERVES 6 AS PART OF A SHARED MEAL

Cut the bitter melon in half, remove the insides, and discard them. Cut the flesh into ½–¾ inch (1–2 cm) thick rounds and put them in a colander. Add ½ teaspoon of the turmeric, ½ teaspoon of salt, and the lime juice to the bitter melon. Leave in the colander over a plate, as the melon will release some water, for 20 minutes. (You can discard this water, but it is also used in India as a medicine to control diabetes.)

Fill a wok or heavy-based saucepan one-third full with oil, and heat to 355°F (180°C), or until a cube of bread turns golden brown in 15 seconds. Deep-fry half of the onion until crisp. Remove with a slotted spoon and drain on a paper towel. Set aside. These will be used to finish the dish.

Ensure the oil in the wok is still at 355°F. Roll the bitter melon in the chickpea flour and deep-fry for 3–4 minutes or until golden. Remove with a slotted spoon and drain on a paper towel. Set aside.

Heat 3 tablespoons of oil in a large frying pan over medium heat, add the cumin seeds, and brown. Add the remaining uncooked onion and cook until brown. Add the asafetida, chili powder, green chili, and palm sugar and cook for 3 minutes, sprinkling with a little bit of water to prevent the mixture burning.

Add the bitter melon crisps and toss quickly. Sprinkle with the amchur and garnish with the cilantro leaves and fried onion.

chicken 65

This dish originated in a famous eatery in Chennai called Buhari. The true origin of the number "65" is highly debated. According to the most prevalent theory, it was the 65th item on a long menu, but another common anecdote is that the dish uses a chicken that has been raised for 65 days.

1 tablespoon finely grated ginger

1 tablespoon crushed garlic

1½ tablespoons red chili powder

juice of 1½ limes

3 eggs, lightly beaten

1 lb 9 oz (700 g) skinless chicken thigh fillets, cut into bite-sized pieces

3 tablespoons all-purpose flour

vegetable or sunflower oil, for deep-frying

20 curry leaves

finely shredded ginger, to garnish

green chutney (see page 210), to serve (optional)

SERVES 4 AS PART OF A SHARED MEAL

Combine the finely grated ginger, garlic, chili powder, lime juice, and eggs in a shallow dish. Add the chicken and mix well. Leave to marinate in the fridge for 30 minutes. The longer you allow the chicken to marinate, the more the flavors will infuse into the chicken.

Remove the chicken from the marinade, allowing any excess to drip off. Dust the chicken lightly with the flour.

Fill a wok or heavy-based saucepan one-third full with oil, and heat to 355°F (180°C) or until a cube of bread turns golden brown in 15 seconds. Deep-fry the chicken for about 3 minutes, or until golden brown and cooked through. Remove with a slotted spoon and drain on a paper towel. Put in a serving dish.

In the same oil, deep-fry the curry leaves until crispy—this will happen very quickly, about 20 seconds. Remove with a slotted spoon and drain on a paper towel.

Crush half of the fried curry leaves and scatter over the fried chicken. Garnish the chicken with the remaining fried curry leaves and the ginger, and serve with the chutney.

thengai erachi

beef chili coconut fry

This dish is from the Syrian Christian community in the South Indian state of Kerala. The coconut with fennel and the garam masala and pepper work well together. The beef is a robust enough meat to stand up to the strong spices. The cooking medium is coconut oil, which is found in abundance in this region of India. Keralan cuisine uses the coconut as well as a lot of spice, as the region has been a major spice trade center for centuries.

½ teaspoon ground turmeric

2 teaspoons ground coriander

1 teaspoon ground cumin

½ teaspoon ground fennel

½ teaspoon garam masala
(see page 125)

1 lb 5 oz (600 g) beef sirloin
or rump steak, cut into
finger-sized strips

2 tablespoons vegetable oil

6 curry leaves

½ cup (3½ fl oz/100 ml) coconut
oil (see glossary)

4 dried red chilies

2-inch (5-cm) piece of cassia bark
(see glossary)

1 large onion, sliced

6 garlic cloves, sliced

½ teaspoon cracked black pepper

1½ teaspoons finely grated ginger

3 tablespoons coconut flakes
or shredded coconut, toasted

SERVES 4–6 AS PART OF A SHARED MEAL

Combine the turmeric, coriander, cumin, fennel, and garam masala in a bowl. Add the beef and toss to coat in the spices. Set aside to marinate for 30 minutes.

Heat the oil in a frying pan over low heat, add the curry leaves, and fry until just crisp. Drain on a paper towel and set aside.

Heat 3 tablespoons of the coconut oil in a wok over medium heat, add the chilies and cassia bark, and cook for 1 minute. Add the onion and cook for 5 minutes or until softened. Add the garlic and pepper and cook for 1 minute. Add the ginger and cook for 1 minute.

Heat the remaining coconut oil in a separate large frying pan over high heat and sear the beef, in two batches. This is to prevent the beef from releasing too much moisture.

Once all the beef is cooked, add it to the wok, with the coconut flakes and fried curry leaves. Mix quickly, season with salt, and serve.

kothu kari

stir-fried chopped lamb

*Kothu in Tamil means "chopped." The technique uses
two cleavers—one in each hand—to chop the meat.*

1 lb 5 oz (600 g) lamb shoulder

7 oz (200 g) lamb backstrap

**7 tablespoons (3½ fl oz/100 ml)
vegetable or sunflower oil**

1 teaspoon black mustard seeds

2 onions, chopped

1 tablespoon finely grated ginger

1 tablespoon crushed garlic

1 teaspoon ground fennel

**2 teaspoons ground
black pepper**

1 teaspoon ground turmeric

2 teaspoons red chili powder

1 tablespoon ground coriander

juice of 1 lime

10 curry leaves

SERVES 4–6 AS PART OF A SHARED MEAL

Put both cuts of lamb on a chopping board and, using two cleavers, dice into ½–¾ inch (1–2 cm) cubes using a chopping action. The diced meat should be chopped, but not minced.

Heat 2 tablespoons of the oil in a large wok over high heat, add the lamb in batches, and stir-fry for 1 minute. Remove from the wok and set aside.

Heat the remaining oil in the wok, add the mustard seeds and let them crackle for about 20 seconds. Add the onion, ginger, and garlic and stir-fry for about 3 minutes or until lightly browned.

Return the lamb to the wok, then stir in the fennel, pepper, turmeric, chili powder, and coriander, and stir-fry until the meat is cooked. Drizzle over the lime juice, stir in the curry leaves, and serve.

chicken harra masala

coriander & mint chicken

A North Indian favorite, with the freshness of green herbs and background notes of spices.
These make the dish very fresh, light, and crisp in taste. The "harra" refers to the color, meaning green.
It's best to cook the dish without a lid, which will help to retain the color.

vegetable or sunflower oil,
for deep-frying

3 onions, thinly sliced

8 small green chilies

1 bunch mint, leaves picked

1 bunch cilantro (coriander),
leaves picked

⅓ cup (1¾ oz/50 g) cashews

½ cup (4½ oz/130 g) plain
thick yogurt, beaten

2 teaspoons finely grated ginger

2 teaspoons crushed garlic

2 lb 4 oz (1 kg) boneless, skinless
chicken thigh fillets, cut into
1½-inch (4-cm) pieces

1-inch (2.5-cm) piece of
cinnamon stick

4 green cardamom pods

8 black peppercorns

1 teaspoon cumin seeds

2 teaspoons coriander seeds

3 tablespoons ghee
(see glossary)

¼ teaspoon ground turmeric

2 tablespoons half-and-half cream
(18% fat)

cherry tomato quarters and ginger
slices, to garnish

SERVES 6–8 AS PART OF A SHARED MEAL

Fill a wok or heavy-based saucepan one-third full with oil, and heat to 355°F (180°C) or until a cube of bread turns golden brown in 15 seconds. Deep-fry the onion until crisp. Remove with a slotted spoon and drain on a paper towel. Reserve some to garnish.

Grind the green chilies, mint leaves, coriander leaves, cashews, and remaining fried onion together in a food processor to make a smooth paste. This is your green masala.

Combine the yogurt, ginger, garlic, and green masala in a large bowl. Add the chicken and mix well to coat. Leave to marinate in the fridge for 30 minutes.

Meanwhile, put the cinnamon, cardamom, peppercorns, and cumin and coriander seeds in a spice grinder and grind to a fine powder. This is your powdered masala. Set aside.

Heat the ghee in a large frying pan over medium–high heat, add the chicken, and sear on all sides. Add the turmeric and 1 cup (8 fl oz/250 ml) of water, and season with salt. Cook, uncovered, for about 15 minutes.

When the chicken is almost cooked, add the powdered masala and cream, and simmer for 5 minutes or until the chicken is cooked through and the sauce is smooth and rich. Ladle into a serving dish and garnish with the reserved fried onions, cherry tomato, and ginger.

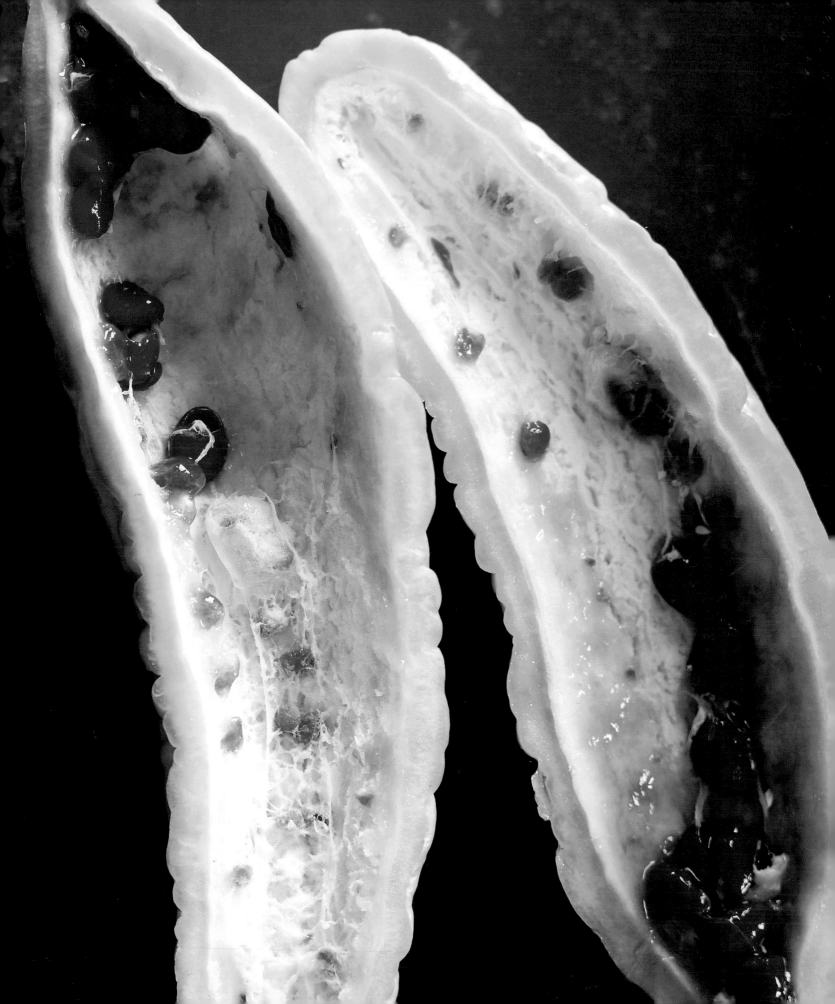

rajastani laal maas

fiery goat curry

This is a very spicy dish from the deserts of Rajasthan. It's marked by a striking red color from the chilies. A chili paste is made from soaked whole chilies, which gives it a very different taste from red chili powder. Also, ghee is used instead of oil to balance the heat of the chilies. This dish is unusual as it does not use ginger or tomato.

20 dried red chilies

1 teaspoon cumin seeds

½ cup (4½ oz/130 g) Greek-style yogurt

½ teaspoon ground turmeric

2 tablespoons ground coriander

7 tablespoons (3½ oz/100 g) ghee (see glossary)

6 garlic cloves, sliced

6 green cardamom pods

3 black cardamom pods

2 onions, thinly sliced

2 lb 12 oz (1.25 kg) goat leg or shoulder shank, bone in, cubed (ask your butcher to do this for you)

SERVES 6 AS PART OF A SHARED MEAL

Soak the dried chilies in warm water for 20 minutes to soften. Drain and reserve 4 chilies for later. Process the remainder to a fine paste in a blender.

Heat a frying pan over high heat and dry-fry the cumin seeds for about 1 minute, shaking the pan regularly. Finely crush the seeds using a mortar and pestle.

Combine the yogurt with the turmeric, ground coriander, chili paste, and crushed cumin seeds in a bowl and set aside.

Heat the ghee in a large heavy-based saucepan over medium–high heat, add the garlic and cook for 2 minutes or until golden brown. Add the green and black cardamom pods and the reserved chilies, stir, then add the onion and cook for 6–8 minutes or until brown.

Add the goat and cook for 4–5 minutes, stirring to coat in the onion. Add the yogurt mixture with 3 cups (26 fl oz/750 ml) of water, bring to a boil, then reduce the heat to low and cook, uncovered, stirring occasionally, for about 2 hours or until the meat is tender. Check the seasoning and serve hot.

rava methi machi

semolina-crusted salmon

juice of 1 lime

1 teaspoon finely grated ginger

1 teaspoon crushed garlic

1 lb 5 oz (600 g) salmon fillets,
skin on, cut into 2¾ oz–3½ oz
(80–100 g) portions

½ cup (3¼ oz/95 g) coarse
semolina

3 tablespoons all-purpose flour

1 tablespoon dried fenugreek
leaves (see glossary)

½ teaspoon ground cumin

¼ teaspoon ground turmeric

½ teaspoon red chili powder

3 tablespoons vegetable
or sunflower oil

tamarind and ginger chutney
(see page 210), to serve

SERVES 6 AS PART OF A SHARED MEAL
Combine the lime juice, ginger, and garlic, brush the mixture all
over the salmon and set aside to marinate for 30 minutes.

Combine the semolina, flour, fenugreek leaves, cumin, turmeric,
and chili powder. Heavily coat the salmon in the flour mixture.

Heat the oil in a large frying pan over medium–high heat, add
the salmon skin-side down, and cook until the skin is crisp, then
turn over and cook for another 2–3 minutes or until the fish is just
cooked through—do not overcook the salmon; it should be pink
and soft in the middle. Serve with the tamarind and ginger chutney.

aatukal karaikudi

lamb karaikuidi

3 tablespoons vegetable or
sunflower oil

2 onions, roughly chopped

1 tablespoon coriander seeds

5 dried red chilies

½ teaspoon fennel seeds

2 star anise

1 tablespoon finely grated ginger

1 tablespoon crushed garlic

⅓ cup (3¼ oz/90 g) tomato paste
(concentrated purée)

2 lb 4 oz (1 kg) diced lamb leg

12 curry leaves

parathas, to serve (see glossary)

SERVES 6–8 AS PART OF A SHARED MEAL

Heat 1 tablespoon of the oil in a frying pan over medium heat, add the onion and coriander seeds, and cook for 6–8 minutes or until the onion is brown. Cool, then put into a spice grinder and blend to a smooth paste.

Heat the remaining oil in a large saucepan over medium heat. Add the red chilies, fennel, star anise, ginger, and garlic, and cook for 2 minutes.

Add the onion paste and stir to combine well with the spices, then add the tomato paste and cook for 3 minutes.

Add the lamb and 2 cups (17 fl oz/500 ml) of water, reduce the heat to low and cook, covered, for 30 minutes. This dish should not have a flowing gravy, so if the sauce is still thin after cooking, increase the heat to high and cook, uncovered, for about 5 minutes, or until the sauce has reduced to a thick consistency. Stir in the curry leaves and serve with the parathas.

karara bhindi

crispy okra

Okra are also called "ladies' fingers" in India due to their curved shape. They are a rich source of dietary fiber, minerals, and vitamins, and they are thought to enhance brain power. Prior to school exams okra is a prime vegetable that gets added to a lot of dishes—this is an ancient natural remedy that existed before such things as memory-boosting tablets came onto the market.

Okra is a naturally slimy vegetable that requires the right cooking technique, as shown in this recipe, to achieve the perfect texture and taste. These crispy snacks are an excellent accompaniment to a chilled beer on a summer afternoon. We serve this at Aki's as a starter.

1 lb 2 oz (500 g) okra, cut into strips

½ teaspoon red chili powder

¼ teaspoon ground turmeric

juice of 1 lime

vegetable or sunflower oil, for deep-frying

1 cup (4¼ oz/120 g) chickpea flour (besan)

½ cup (2¾ oz/80 g) rice flour

½ teaspoon cumin seeds

2 teaspoons finely grated ginger

date and tamarind chutney (see page 108) or burrani raita (see page 211), to serve

SERVES 4 AS PART OF A SHARED MEAL

Lightly season the okra with the chili powder, turmeric, and lime juice. Do not marinate it for too long because the okra will leach its stickiness and make it very difficult to dust with the flour.

Fill a wok or large saucepan one-third full with oil, and heat to about 355°F (180°C), or until a cube of bread turns golden brown in 15 seconds. Combine the chickpea and rice flours, cumin seeds, ginger, and a little salt in a bowl. Dust the okra in the flour mixture. Deep-fry the okra, in batches, for 2–3 minutes or until golden brown and crisp, turning once to cook evenly. Remove with a slotted spoon and drain on a paper towel. Serve immediately with the chutney or raita.

shahi tukda

mughal bread & butter pudding

This is essentially a glorified bread and butter pudding from the royal Mughal kitchens. The origin of this dish is Lucknow in Uttar Pradesh. In Urdu, shahi means "royal" and tukda means "bits," and refers to how the royal cooks would use the plethora of breads left over from the emperor's meals to prepare this dessert. This pudding is pure indulgence (and will ensure you need a couple of hours on the treadmill!). Traditionally, to showcase the richness of Mughlai cuisine, chandi warq (edible silver leaf) is used to decorate dishes. This is still made in the traditional manner where small pieces of silver are placed between two sheets of paper and hammered out until it is papery thin. The silver leaf is pure fancy and adds to the opulence of the dish.

8 saffron threads

6 teaspoons (1 fl oz/30 ml) rosewater

2 cups (17 fl oz/500 ml) milk

6 slices white bread, crusts removed

½ cup (4½ oz/125 g) ghee, melted (see glossary)

1 cup (7 oz/200 g) granulated sugar

honey, for drizzling

1 sheet edible silver leaf (optional)

vanilla bean ice cream, to serve (optional)

SERVES 6 AS A DESSERT

Preheat the oven to 350°F (180°C/Gas 4).

Soak 3 saffron threads in 5 teaspoons (1 fl oz/25 ml) of the rosewater to make a saffron rosewater for serving. Set aside.

Put the milk in a heavy-based stainless-steel saucepan and bring to a boil over low heat, stirring constantly. Continue gently simmering, scraping the sides and base of the pan to ensure the milk doesn't burn, until the milk has reduced to one-third. Set aside to cool. This is called the rabri.

Cut each slice of bread in half to make triangles, and toast in the oven for 10 minutes, then brush each side with the melted ghee, return to the oven, and toast for 15 minutes or until crisp and golden. Set aside.

Meanwhile, put the sugar in a saucepan with 1¾ cups (14 fl oz/400 ml) of water, bring to a boil, then simmer for 10 minutes to make a syrup. Add the remaining saffron and the remaining teaspoon of rosewater. Remove from the heat.

Place the bread triangles in the hot sugar syrup and leave until well soaked.

To serve, arrange two bread triangles on each plate and pour over the rabri. Drizzle with the honey and the saffron rosewater. Using a knife, carefully remove a small piece of the silver leaf and put on each dish. Serve with a scoop of ice cream if desired.

sour

SOUR AWAKENS THE SPIRIT and sharpens the mind. Sourness sharpens flavors. It stimulates the taste buds, and according to Ayurvedic beliefs it has a "wake-up" quality, which brings us back to reality.

After I finished cooking college I landed a position at the Taj Mahal Palace Hotel in Bombay (now Mumbai). I was only seventeen and after the bitter struggle with my parents over my decision to become a chef, a job at a prestigious hotel in a big cosmopolitan city such as Bombay was exactly what I needed. It was my own "wake-up" to reality, to forget the hardships I had endured to get there. My life was finally taking shape. The Taj was the first of many wake-up calls. I journeyed all over the subcontinent and further afield to the Sheraton in Iraq, and was sent by the Indian government as a culinary ambassador to Australia. It was the "sour" I had been looking for to balance the "bitter."

Sour foods are ideal for summer (along with salty, while in winter the flavors should shift to pungent and salty).

The original souring agents in Indian cooking were tamarind, green mango, and kokam. They often act as preservatives, and sourness plays an important part in pickling. Tamarind is an essential part of any Tamil fish curry, especially as people didn't have refrigeration in the past. Villagers would make their curry in a clay pot and the tamarind helped keep it fresh for a day or two—and as we all know, curry always tastes better the next day.

Kokam, which comes from the west coast and is part of the mangosteen family, has both medicinal and culinary uses and nearly all of the plant is used, mostly as a garnish for curries. You can find the fruit, oil, and syrup in Australia. The fruit, which has a deep red beet color, has a sweet, acidic taste (and antiseptic qualities) when fresh, but the flavor is tart when used dried, while the bark and leaves also have a more astringent flavor.

The gandhraj lemon is native to Kolkata (Calcutta) and has a distinct sour flavor I love.

When I sit down at the table, no meal is complete without a chutney or pickle. Chutneys and pickles are an excellent combination of sweet, sour, salty, and sometimes chili that brings everything alive and reinvigorates the palate. Mango pickles are an essential part of any meal. Green mango has a sour quality that provides an important contrast to the richness of a curry.

mango oysters

Every year in July we celebrate Abhi's anniversary with a new theme and food from a particular region of India. The reason for this is to take the customers on a tasty journey through the country's different regions. Traveling to various parts of India to discover the variety of food that exists has become a new tradition for Suba and me. Customers showed their interest in knowing about the differences in regional cooking, and that encouraged us to broaden and deepen our knowledge of Indian food. The new discoveries kept Abhi's moving in a direction of traditional yet contemporary Indian cuisine. This is one of the hits from an Abhi's anniversary dinner. This is a fresh and flavorful dressing with an Indian bent. It is quite versatile; try it on ceviche. The dressing can be made in advance.

1 green mango, peeled and finely diced

1 tablespoon amchur (dry mango powder) (see glossary) or 1 tablespoon lime juice (optional)

1 tablespoon finely grated ginger

2 tablespoons finely chopped cilantro (coriander), plus baby leaves to garnish

1 teaspoon granulated sugar

24 oysters, shucked and on the half shell

SERVES 4 AS A STARTER

You will need to begin this recipe a day ahead.

If the mango is not sour enough for your taste, sprinkle with the amchur or lime juice. Put the mango in a bowl, add 1 teaspoon of salt, and let it marinate in the fridge overnight. This will make the mango release its juices, which are quite acidic. Do not drain the juices.

Squeeze the juice from the ginger into a small bowl and discard the ginger. Add the cilantro and sugar to the ginger juice and stir to dissolve the sugar.

Add to the mango. Spoon over the oysters and serve garnished with the baby cilantro leaves.

brinjal mirchi salan

eggplant & chili curry

A Hyderabadi (South Indian) delight. Hyderabad possesses a good fusion of Mughlai and Southern Indian cooking. The Nawabs of Hyderabad adapted the Mughlai cuisine to suit the region in which they found themselves.

8 baby eggplants

1½ teaspoons ground turmeric

⅓ cup (2½ fl oz/80 ml) vegetable or sunflower oil

1 teaspoon panch phoran masala (see glossary)

2 red onions, thinly sliced

10 curry leaves

1 tablespoon finely grated ginger

2 teaspoons crushed garlic

2 tablespoons ground coriander

1½ tablespoons Kashmiri chili powder (see glossary)

2 tablespoons tamarind pulp (see glossary)

2 long green bell peppers, cut into 1-inch (2.5-cm) slices

fried curry leaves, to garnish

finely shredded ginger, to garnish

MASALA PASTE

⅓ cup (1¾ oz/50 g) raw peanuts, skins off

1 oz (25 g) sesame seeds

2¾ oz (80 g) shredded coconut

4 small green chilies, chopped

SERVES 4–6 AS PART OF A SHARED MEAL

To make the masala paste, heat a medium frying pan over medium heat, add the peanuts, sesame seeds, and coconut, and dry-fry them until lightly toasted, shaking the pan regularly. Transfer to a small blender or spice grinder with the green chilies and process or grind to a smooth paste. Gradually add ½ cup (4 fl oz/125 ml) of water and process or grind until smooth and combined. Set aside.

Slice a deep cross in the base of each eggplant (slicing up about half the length of each), rub a bit of salt and ½ teaspoon of the turmeric among the eggplants into the cuts and leave for 20–30 minutes.

Heat 2 tablespoons of the oil in a medium saucepan over medium heat, add the panch phoran masala, onion, and curry leaves, and cook until the onion is golden brown. Add the ginger and garlic and cook for 1 minute. Add 2 tablespoons of water and the coriander, chili powder, and remaining turmeric, and cook for 2 minutes. Add the tamarind pulp, masala paste, and 4 cups (35 fl oz/1 liter) of water, and cook for 20 minutes over low heat.

Meanwhile, heat the remaining oil in a frying pan over medium–high heat, add the eggplant, and fry until lightly golden and seared on all sides.

Once the sauce is cooked, add the eggplants and cook for about 10 minutes or until the eggplants are soft. Season with salt, add the capsicum, and cook for 5 minutes—the capsicum does not need to be cooked for too long. Garnish with the curry leaves and ginger to serve.

Tip: To get a smooth paste while grinding, do not add too much water at one time. To increase the heat and sharpness, slit a green chili and throw it in the mix toward the end with some curry leaves.

pakodi kadi

fried dumplings with yogurt sauce

A summery Sunday afternoon lunch with the family is the perfect occasion for kadi to be made. All regions of India have a version of kadi, which is usually made from yogurt when it starts to go sour. The Gujaratis add some sugar to it, while Southern Indians will add ground coconut, but regardless of the region, the one essential ingredient in a kadi is asafetida. It can be made lighter if the fried dumplings are omitted. The perfect accompaniments are white rice, pappadoms, and mango pickle. This is a favorite of my restaurant staff and of mine, especially when my young chef Dhanasekaran cooks it.

PAKODI

1 small onion, chopped

1 cup (4¼ oz/120 g) chickpea
flour (besan)

⅛ teaspoon carom seeds (ajwain)
(see glossary)

⅛ teaspoon baking soda

2 tablespoons fine rice flour

1 teaspoon finely chopped
cilantro (coriander)

¼ teaspoon finely grated ginger

¼ teaspoon red chili powder

⅛ teaspoon ground turmeric

¼ teaspoon coriander seeds, crushed

vegetable or sunflower oil,
for deep-frying

KADI

scant 2 cups (1 lb 2 oz/500 g)
plain thick yogurt

2 tablespoons vegetable or sunflower oil

⅓ cup (1½ oz/40 g) chickpea flour
(besan)

2 teaspoons finely grated ginger

½ bunch cilantro (coriander), stalks
only, finely chopped

1½ teaspoons red chili powder

1 teaspoon ground turmeric

⅛ teaspoon asafetida (see glossary)

TEMPERING

2 tablespoons vegetable or sunflower oil

¼ teaspoon black mustard seeds

1 dried red chili

1 teaspoon coriander seeds

1 teaspoon cumin seeds

⅛ teaspoon asafetida (see glossary)

1 sprig of curry leaves, leaves picked (optional)

To make the pakodi, combine all of the ingredients, except the oil, with ½ cup (4 fl oz/125 ml) of water, season with salt, and set aside for 10 minutes.

Fill a wok or heavy-based saucepan one-third full with oil, and heat to 340°F (170°C), or until a cube of bread turns golden brown in 20 seconds.

To make the pakodi, wet your fingers with oil or water as the mixture is quite sticky, then take small amounts (about a level dessert spoon) and form into small dumplings. Carefully drop into the oil as you make them. Deep-fry the pakodi for about 3–4 minutes or until golden brown, but not crisp. Remove with a slotted spoon and drain on a paper towel. You should have about 18 pakodi. Set aside.

To make the kadi, put all of the ingredients in a medium saucepan over medium heat and cook for 20 minutes, stirring very regularly so the yogurt does not separate.

Add the fried pakodi, stirring to coat in the sauce, and cook for 5 minutes. Remove from the heat.

To make the tempering, heat the oil in a small frying pan over medium–high heat, add the mustard seeds and let them crackle for about 20 seconds. Add the remaining ingredients, except the curry leaves, and cook for 1 minute, then add the curry leaves. Pour this hot tempering carefully (as it may splash) into the kadi just prior to serving.

Serve hot.

chicken cafreal

green chicken curry

Each region of India makes a green chicken curry, and everyone has their own trick to "green it up." This cafreal is a Portuguese-influenced curry from Goa that uses rum—a typical addition in Goan cooking—along with wine, but no other region of India uses alcohol in their cooking. The distinctive use of dark rum and cilantro makes the finished color of this dish a dark bottle green.

2 teaspoons ground turmeric

1 tablespoon finely grated ginger

2 teaspoons crushed garlic

1 tablespoon malt vinegar

2 lb 4 oz (1 kg) skinless, boneless chicken thigh fillets, each cut into thirds

⅓ cup (2½ fl oz/80 ml) vegetable or sunflower oil

chili oil, to garnish (optional)

GREEN MASALA PASTE

1 bunch cilantro (coriander), leaves picked

½ bunch mint, leaves picked

1 onion, chopped

4 small green chilies

2-inch (5-cm) piece of ginger

1 tablespoon granulated sugar

6 garlic cloves

2-inch (5-cm) piece of cinnamon stick

12 black peppercorns

6 whole cloves

2 teaspoons cumin seeds

3 tablespoons dark rum

2 tablespoons malt vinegar

Combine the turmeric, ginger, garlic, vinegar, and ½ teaspoon of salt in a bowl, rub all over the chicken and leave to marinate in the fridge for 1 hour.

To make the green masala paste, put all of the ingredients in a blender or spice grinder and process to a fine paste. Heat the oil in a large heavy-based frying pan over medium–high heat, add the chicken, and cook until golden brown on all sides.

Add the green masala paste and cook, covered, over low heat for 15–20 minutes or until the chicken is cooked through, removing the lid for the final 3 minutes of cooking to reduce the sauce slightly, if necessary. Drizzle with the chili oil to serve.

paneer matar bhurji

cheese & peas curry

I discovered this dish at a small eatery called Kailash Parbat on Colaba Causeway in Mumbai (Bombay). It became my regular dining place on my days off from the Taj Mahal Palace Hotel. It was quite popular among the hotel staff at that time. That eatery continues to this day and you can still spot the odd chef from the Taj, enjoying his vegetarian meal.

3 tablespoons ghee, melted
(see glossary)

½ teaspoon cumin seeds

3 small green chilies, chopped

1 onion, finely chopped

1 tablespoon finely grated ginger

¼ teaspoon ground turmeric

1 teaspoon ground coriander

½ teaspoon dried fenugreek leaves
(see glossary)

1 tomato, finely diced

10½ oz (300 g) paneer
(curd cheese) (see glossary),
crumbled, or cottage cheese

⅔ cup (3½ oz/100 g) green peas

3 tablespoons half-and-half cream
(18% fat)

3 cilantro (coriander) sprigs,
leaves picked

rotis (see glossary) or chapatis
(see page 218), to serve

SERVES 4 AS PART OF A SHARED MEAL

Heat the ghee in a heavy-based saucepan over medium heat, add the cumin seeds, and fry for 1 minute until brown. Add the chili and cook for 1 minute. Add the onion and cook for 6–8 minutes, or until brown. Add the ginger, turmeric, ground coriander, fenugreek leaves, and tomato, and cook for 5 minutes.

Add the paneer and peas, and cook, covered, for 5–7 minutes. Stir through the cream, season with salt, and remove from the heat.

Garnish with the cilantro leaves and serve hot. Serve with rotis or chapatis.

beef jardaloo

beef with apricots

This is a classic festive Parsi dish that I picked up during my time in Mumbai (Bombay). Parsi cooking has a heavy Persian influence, hence the use of dried fruit. This sweet, tangy, and spicy dish is best enjoyed with either chapatis or a pilaf.

1¼ cups (7 oz/200 g) dried apricots

4 cinnamon sticks

6 green cardamom pods

4 whole cloves

5 dried red chilies

2 teaspoons cumin seeds

2 teaspoons coriander seeds

2 tablespoons (1 fl oz/30 ml) malt vinegar

2 tablespoons sunflower oil

2 onions, chopped

½ teaspoon garam masala (see page 125)

2 tomatoes, chopped

1 lb 5 oz (600 g) beef rump steak, cubed

½ bunch cilantro (coriander), leaves roughly chopped

SERVES 4 AS PART OF A SHARED MEAL

Soak the apricots in 1 cup (8 fl oz/250 ml) of water, preferably overnight. Otherwise, soak in warm water for about 3 hours or until soft and swollen. Drain and set aside.

Put two of the cinnamon sticks in a spice grinder with the cardamom pods, cloves, dried chilies, and cumin and coriander seeds, and grind to a fine powder. Add the vinegar and 1 tablespoon of water, and blend to a paste. Set aside.

Heat the oil in a saucepan over medium heat, add the remaining cinnamon sticks and the onion, and cook for 6–8 minutes or until the onion is brown.

Add the garam masala and the spice paste, and cook, sprinkling over a little water so the spices don't burn, for 1–2 minutes or until you see the oil separating on the sides.

Add the tomato and cook for 2–3 minutes.

Add the beef and apricots and gently cook, covered, for about 30–40 minutes or until the beef is tender. Season with salt and garnish with the chopped cilantro.

chatpata machli

tangy seared fish

½ teaspoon ground turmeric

1 tablespoon red chili powder, plus extra for dusting

1 teaspoon ground black pepper

1 tablespoon coconut oil

1 teaspoon black mustard seeds

½ teaspoon fenugreek seeds

6 French shallots (eschalots), chopped

3 garlic cloves, sliced

10 tablespoons (5 fl oz/150 ml) tamarind water (see glossary)

¾ cup (7 fl oz/200 ml) coconut milk

1 lb 12 oz (800 g) snapper fillets

1 orange sweet potato

vegetable or sunflower oil, for deep-frying

1 tablespoon chopped cilantro (coriander)

Combine the turmeric, chili powder, and pepper with about 1 tablespoon of water to make a smooth paste.

Heat the coconut oil in a heavy-based saucepan over medium heat, add the mustard seeds and fenugreek seeds and let them crackle for about 20 seconds. Add the shallot and garlic, and cook for 1 minute. Add the turmeric paste and cook for 2 minutes.

Stir in the tamarind water, season with salt, and cook over low heat for 10 minutes.

Add the coconut milk and simmer for 2–3 minutes or until you have a thick paste. Remove from the heat and cool to room temperature.

Once cool, reserve 3 tablespoons of the mixture. Spread the remaining mixture all over the fish and put in the fridge to marinate for at least 2 hours.

While the fish is marinating, prepare the garnish. Peel and cut the sweet potato into matchstick-sized pieces. Fill a wok or heavy-based saucepan one-third full with oil, and heat to 355°F (180°C) or until a cube of bread turns golden brown in 15 seconds. Fry the sweet potato matchsticks until crisp. Remove with a slotted spoon and drain on a paper towel, then dust lightly with salt and chili powder.

Heat the reserved coconut milk mixture with 2 tablespoons of water to make a sauce to drizzle over the fish.

Preheat a barbecue grill plate or chargrill pan to medium–high. Cook the fish for about 2 minutes each side or until cooked through.

Serve the fish with a little of the sauce drizzled over and garnished with the sweet potato matchsticks and coriander.

goan fish curry

2 lb 4 oz (1 kg) whole barramundi (or other firm white-fleshed fish), skin on, cut into finger-sized pieces, about ¾ inch (2 cm) wide

½ teaspoon ground turmeric

5 pieces of kokam (see glossary) or extra 1 tablespoon of tamarind pulp

1 long red chili

3 tablespoons vegetable or sunflower oil

1 onion, sliced

1 teaspoon finely grated ginger

½ teaspoon crushed garlic

1 tablespoon tamarind pulp (see glossary)

3½ tablespoons (1½ fl oz/50 ml) coconut cream

2 teaspoons fincly shredded ginger, to garnish

MASALA PASTE

1 cup (5 oz/140 g) grated coconut or 1⅔ cups (5½ oz/150 g) shredded coconut (see glossary)

8 Kashmiri dried red chilies (see glossary) or 1½ tablespoons sweet paprika

1 tablespoon coriander seeds

2 teaspoons cumin seeds

1 teaspoon black peppercorns

1 teaspoon ground turmeric

SERVES 6 AS PART OF A SHARED MEAL

Rub the fish with the turmeric and set aside for about 30 minutes. Soak the kokam in 1 cup (8 fl oz/250 ml) of hot water for about 10 minutes.

Prepare a chili flower for garnish. Cut a cross in the bottom half of the red chili and leave it in icy cold water for 5 minutes.

To make the masala paste, put all of the ingredients in a spice grinder and grind to a fine paste. Add ½ cup (4 fl oz/125 ml) of water and process into a smooth, fine paste.

Heat the oil in a large heavy-based saucepan over medium heat, add the onion, and cook for 5 minutes. Add the ginger and garlic, and cook for 2 minutes.

Add the masala paste and cook for 2 minutes.

Add the kokam and its soaking water and the tamarind pulp and simmer for 15 minutes over low heat.

Add the coconut cream and fish, and cook for 5 minutes or until the fish is cooked. Garnish with the chili flower and shredded ginger.

Tip: To get some extra flavor, marinate the fish with salt and chili powder along with the ground turmeric.

crispy pork with ginger tamarind glaze

This dish appeared on the very first Abhi's menu. It was a special request from my dear friend Tava. It has since become a favorite dish for quite a few of our regulars. It also makes a nice starter without the glaze.

RUB

1½ tablespoons coriander seeds, crushed

1½ tablespoons finely grated ginger

2 teaspoons cracked black pepper

2 teaspoons crushed garlic

1 teaspoon fennel seeds

½ teaspoon ground turmeric

1 teaspoon red chili powder

1 teaspoon garam masala (see page 125)

juice of 1 lime

1 lb 7 oz (650 g) boneless pork belly, sliced

⅓ cup (1½ oz/40 g) chickpea flour (besan)

3 tablespoons corn flour (cornstarch)

vegetable or sunflower oil, for shallow-frying

2-inch (5-cm) piece of ginger, finely shredded

1 long red chili, finely shredded

1 small green chili, finely shredded

GINGER TAMARIND GLAZE

1 tablespoon vegetable oil

½ teaspoon black mustard seeds

2 teaspoons finely grated ginger

2 tablespoons tamarind pulp

2 tablespoons grated palm sugar (jaggery) or soft brown sugar

Combine all of the rub ingredients and season with salt. Rub all over the pork and set aside for 20 minutes.

Combine the chickpea flour and corn flour and season lightly with salt.

Heat the oil in a large frying pan over medium heat, dust the pork in the flour mixture, shaking off the excess, add to the pan, and shallow-fry for about 6 minutes, turning regularly until crisp. Drain on a paper towel, then cut into finger-sized strips. Set aside.

To make the ginger tamarind glaze, heat the oil in a saucepan over medium–high heat, add the mustard seeds and let them crackle for 20 seconds. Add the ginger, tamarind, sugar, and 3 tablespoons of water, bring to a boil, and reduce until the sauce is a coating consistency.

Add the fried pork strips to the glaze and toss to coat. Garnish with the ginger and chili.

patrani machi

fish steamed in banana leaves

1 lb 12 oz (800 g) blue-eye trevalla fillets, cut into 4–6 portions

1 teaspoon ground turmeric

2–3 banana leaves

1 bunch cilantro (coriander), roughly chopped

½ bunch mint, roughly chopped

2 small green chilies, roughly chopped

2-inch (5-cm) piece of ginger, roughly chopped

1 cup (3¼ oz/90 g) shredded coconut

2 teaspoons store-bought mango chutney

½ teaspoon cumin seeds

juice of 1–2 limes

6–8 black peppercorns

lime wedges, to serve

SERVES 4–6 AS PART OF A SHARED MEAL

Rub the fish with the turmeric and set aside to marinate for 15–20 minutes.

Cut the banana leaves into 4 to 6 squares large enough to enclose a portion of fish. Line a large bamboo or metal steamer basket with parchment paper to prevent sticking.

Put the remaining ingredients, except the lime wedges, in a small blender with ½ teaspoon of salt and process to a coarse paste. Do not grind too finely or you will lose the texture of the coconut.

Put a portion of fish into the center of each banana leaf and apply a thick layer of the paste on top of the fish. Fold the sides of the banana leaf over the fish to completely enclose and put—fold side down—into the steamer basket. Cover with a tight-fitting lid and steam over a saucepan or wok of simmering water for 10–15 minutes, or until the fish is cooked through. Serve immediately in the leaves with the lime wedges.

akoori

curried scrambled eggs

This is my typical start to the day. I can skip lunch or skip dinner but I can't skip akoori! My sons have been trained to make a perfect akoori as well. Much more than curried scrambled eggs, it has flavors that will give you a lift for the whole day. It is as light and energizing as one can ever imagine. Akoori is a traditional Parsi dish, and the trick is to keep the eggs soft and fluffy.

6–8 eggs, lightly beaten

1 tablespoon melted butter

2 tablespoons half-and-half cream (18% fat)

4–5 cilantro (coriander) sprigs, leaves chopped, plus extra to garnish

1 tablespoon vegetable or sunflower oil

1 teaspoon cumin seeds

2 French shallots (eschalots), finely chopped

2 small green chilies, finely chopped with seeds removed

2 teaspoons finely chopped ginger

1 teaspoon finely chopped garlic

¼ teaspoon ground turmeric, plus extra to garnish

1 tomato, finely chopped

toast, to serve

SERVES 4 FOR BREAKFAST

Put the eggs, butter, cream, and cilantro in a bowl, season with salt, and combine.

Heat the oil in a large frying pan over medium heat, add the cumin seeds and allow them to sizzle for 1 minute.

Add the shallot and when almost brown, add the chili, ginger, and garlic, and cook for 1 minute.

Add the turmeric, tomato, and beaten egg mixture and cook over low heat, stirring constantly, until the eggs are cooked to the desired consistency. Check the seasoning and add salt if necessary.

Serve with toast and garnish the plate with the extra cilantro and turmeric.

tip: Remember the eggs will continue to cook even after you remove them from the heat, so it is advisable to remove them a little underdone.

urulai chemeen charu

keralan shrimp curry

This is a very light and simple recipe, greatly enjoyed by the Indian cricket team when they were in Sydney. Chef Biji at Abhi's excels at making this dish, as it is his hometown recipe.

**3 tablespoons vegetable
or sunflower oil**

1 teaspoon black mustard seeds

**10 French shallots (eschalots),
chopped**

1 tablespoon finely grated ginger

2 teaspoons crushed garlic

5 new (baby) potatoes, quartered

4 small green chilies, chopped

2 tomatoes, chopped

**½ cup (2½ oz/70 g) grated coconut
or ½ cup (1½ oz/45 g) shredded
coconut (see glossary)**

**2 tablespoons tamarind pulp
(see glossary)**

12 curry leaves

1 teaspoon red chili powder

½ teaspoon ground turmeric

**1 lb 2 oz (500 g) raw shrimp
(prawns), peeled with tails left
intact and deveined**

SERVES 4 AS PART OF A SHARED MEAL

Heat the oil in a saucepan over medium heat, add the mustard seeds and let them crackle for about 20 seconds. Add the shallot and cook for about 5 minutes, or until softened but not browned. Add the ginger and garlic, and 1 tablespoon of water, and cook for 1 minute.

Add the remaining ingredients, except the shrimp, and cook, covered, over low heat or until the potato is almost cooked. Add the shrimp and cook for 2–3 minutes or until cooked through.

meen pulli kozhambu
tamil fish curry

This is a simple dish of clean flavors. It is a unique Indian dish that does not use any ginger or garlic. The sauce can be made a day before use and kept in the fridge, and the fish curry will always taste better the next day. If available, a terracotta or baked clay pot is the best vessel to cook this fish curry in.

2 lb 4 oz (1 kg) skinless barramundi fillets

½ teaspoon ground turmeric

1 tablespoon Kashmiri chili powder (see glossary)

3 tablespoons vegetable or sunflower oil

1 teaspoon black mustard seeds

2 dried red chilies

¼ teaspoon fenugreek seeds

½ teaspoon cumin seeds

1 large onion, sliced

1 teaspoon red chili powder

2 teaspoons ground coriander

1 teaspoon ground cumin

½ cup (4 fl oz / 125 ml) tamarind water (see glossary)

1 cup (9 oz / 250 g) tomato paste (concentrated purée)

¾ cup (7 fl oz / 200 ml) coconut milk

2 teaspoons granulated sugar (optional)

2 sprigs of curry leaves, leaves picked

SERVES 6 AS PART OF A SHARED MEAL

Rub the fish with the turmeric and half of the Kashmiri chili powder and set aside to marinate for 20 minutes.

Heat the oil in a heavy-based saucepan over medium heat, add the mustard seeds and let them crackle for about 20 seconds. Add the dried chilies, fenugreek, and cumin, and cook for 1 minute or until fragrant, and the tips of the chilies are blackened.

Add the onion and cook over low heat for 6–8 minutes or until the onion is softened but not browned.

Add the red chili powder, remaining Kashmiri chili powder, the coriander, cumin, tamarind, tomato paste, and 1 cup (8 fl oz/ 250 ml) of water, and cook, covered, over low heat for about 15 minutes.

Add the coconut milk and cook for 5 minutes. Taste and, if the tamarind is too sour, add the sugar to balance.

Add the fish and cook for 5 minutes or until the fish is cooked. Season with salt and serve garnished with the curry leaves.

madras prawn vendaki

shrimp & okra curry

¾ cup (3½ oz/100 g) grated
coconut (see glossary)

1 tablespoon roasted chana dal
(see glossary)

⅓ cup (2½ fl oz/80 ml) gingili
(unscented sesame oil)
(see glossary)

2 teaspoons black or brown
mustard seeds

1 teaspoon fenugreek seeds

1 tablespoon cumin seeds

3½ oz (100 g) French shallots
(eschalots), sliced

3½ oz (100 g) okra, trimmed, with a
1¼-inch (3-cm) slit on one side

1 tablespoon red chili powder

2 tablespoons ground coriander

1 teaspoon ground turmeric

⅓ cup (2¼ fl oz/75 ml) tamarind
concentrate (see glossary)

2 tomatoes, diced

12 curry leaves

12 raw jumbo shrimp (prawns),
unpeeled

TEMPERING

1 tablespoon gingili (unscented
sesame oil) (see glossary)

4 dried red chilies

8–10 curry leaves

SERVES 4–6 AS PART OF A SHARED MEAL

Put the coconut and chana dal in a spice grinder and finely grind.
Ensure it is very finely ground—process in batches if necessary.

Heat the gingili in a large heavy-based saucepan over medium
heat, add the mustard seeds and let them crackle for about
20 seconds. Add the fenugreek, cumin, and shallot, and cook for
2 minutes. Add the okra and cook for 5 minutes. Remove the okra
mixture and set aside.

Add the chili powder, coriander, turmeric, tamarind, tomato,
coconut mixture, and 3 cups (26 fl oz/750 ml) of water to the pan
and cook for 5 minutes. Add half of the curry leaves, return the
okra mixture to the pan, and cook for 5 minutes.

Meanwhile, to make the tempering, heat the gingili in a small
frying pan over low heat, add the chilies and curry leaves, and
cook for 1 minute or until fragrant. Remove from the heat.

Once the okra mixture is ready, add the shrimp and cook for
2–3 minutes or until cooked through. Pour the tempering over
the dish and serve immediately.

lagan nu cushter

parsi wedding custard

My dear friend and mentor chef Cyrus Todiwala of Café Spice Namasté in London shares this recipe. I first tasted lagan nu cushter when I joined the Taj Mahal Palace Hotel, Bombay, in 1977 and chef Cyrus was in charge of the kitchen. This custard was not the only sweet surprise waiting for me. At the Taj I had found a mentor in chef Cyrus, who was to become the major influence in my cooking career.

3 cups (26 fl oz/750 ml) milk

2½ cups (21 fl oz/600 ml) half-and-half cream (18% fat)

½ cup (3¾ oz/110 g) granulated sugar

3 eggs

½ teaspoon ground green cardamom

½ teaspoon grated nutmeg

1 tablespoon rosewater

1 vanilla bean, halved lengthwise

2 teaspoons charoli (chironji) (see glossary)

3 pistachio nuts, thinly sliced

2 raw almonds, sliced

butter, to grease

SERVES 8 AS A DESSERT

Preheat the oven to 275°F (140°C/Gas 1).

Put the milk and 1¾ cups (14 fl oz/400 ml) of the cream in a casserole dish or heavy-based saucepan and bring to a boil, remembering that milk overflows very quickly and also burns at the base very rapidly. As soon as it comes to a boil, reduce the heat to a simmer and cook until reduced by roughly half; the color is a lovely pale brown, and it is slightly caramelized. When simmering, one way to avoid losing valuable skin is to constantly brush down the sides of the pan using a wet pastry brush. As the skin forms on the surface, skim it off, reserving for later use.

Once reduced by half, add the sugar and simmer, stirring constantly for 3–5 minutes. Remove from the heat and allow to cool slightly. When it is a bit cooler but still quite warm, put the milk and the collected skin in a blender and blend until smooth.

Put the eggs, remaining cream, the cardamom, nutmeg, and rosewater in a large bowl and scrape in the seeds from the vanilla bean. Blend with an immersion blender to combine. Gradually pour the warm milk into the egg mixture, whisking constantly.

Pour the mixture into eight greased 5-oz (150 ml) capacity ramekins or a greased 6-cup (52 fl oz/1.5 liter) capacity baking dish and sprinkle the nuts over evenly. Sit the ramekins or dish in a roasting tray and fill with water to almost half the height of the dish or ramekins. Bake for about 40 minutes. To check that the custard is cooked, insert a thin small knife in the center; if it comes out clean, the custard is set. Ideally you should also get a nice color on top. Remove from the oven and water bath. Cool to room temperature before serving, or chill to serve.

бебinca

goan layer cake

I tasted this classic Goan dessert for the first time when Abhi's first head chef, Amitava Guha, put it on our menu. It is extremely time consuming to make but the method is simple and the result well worth it.

2 cups (10½ oz/300 g) all-purpose flour

½ teaspoon grated nutmeg

2 cups (15½ fl oz/440 ml) coconut milk

1⅓ cup (8½ oz/240 g) granulated sugar

4 egg yolks

10 green cardamom pods, crushed

2 vanilla beans, halved lengthwise

½ cup (4½ oz/125 g) ghee, melted (see glossary)

vanilla bean ice cream and/or crème anglaise, to serve (optional)

SERVES 6–8 AS A DESSERT

Sift the flour and nutmeg together and set aside. Put the coconut milk, sugar, egg yolks, and cardamom pods in a large bowl and scrape the seeds from the vanilla beans into the bowl. Gently blend using an immersion blender until combined. Strain through a fine sieve into a large bowl.

Fold in the flour mixture to make a smooth batter similar to a pancake batter, adding 2–3 tablespoons of water if the batter seems too thick. The consistency of the batter is the key. Set aside to rest for 45 minutes.

Preheat the oven to 350°F (180°C/Gas 4).

Lightly grease an 8-inch (20-cm) round or square cake pan with the melted ghee and pour in one ladle of batter, just enough to form a ½-inch (1-cm) thick layer, swirling to coat the base of the pan. Bake for 15 minutes or until the top is dark brown. The top part of the layer needs to caramelize before adding the next layer.

Apply some more ghee to the cooked layer before adding the next ladle of batter and bake again. Repeat until you run out of batter (you should end up with about 8 layers). The trick is to get multiple layers but still maintain a cakelike consistency (see tip).

Once the cake is complete, cool and remove from the pan. Slice into triangles and serve warm or cold either with vanilla ice cream and/or crème anglaise.

Tip: You can also cook this under a grill (broiler).

Do not be alarmed if you overbrown a layer, just keep adding the batter, layer by layer. The latter layers will require less cooking time than the first ones.

spice

MARRIAGE IS THE SPICE OF LIFE. Spice brings out the flavor in any dish and is an integral and indispensable part of Indian cuisine. It adds excitement, color, and life.

On July 12, 1987, my destiny and Suba's became entwined. Our marriage was arranged by our families in consultation with an astrologer, so it was already written in the stars for Suba to become an indispensable part of my life—the must-add spice in all my endeavors.

When Indians talk of spice, they're referring to aromatic flavors and not heat. Chili is not a spice. The world of Indian spices is as colorful and varied as the continent itself. It's all about the intricate and delicate use of the right spice for a dish. Masala is a general term for a spice mix and it is the cornerstone of Indian cooking, forming the basis for any good curry. A masala might consist of only two spices or twenty. One of the best known is garam masala (*garam* means "heat") and every region has its own particular version using differing combinations. And, of course, all good cooks have their very own secret recipe.

Spices are India's gift to the world. India grows more than fifty different spices and produces 2.7 million tons annually, accounting for about half the world's spice production. Sangli, in Maharashtra, where Suba once lived and studied, is known as Turmeric City because it has Asia's biggest turmeric-selling market. Pepper, sometimes known as black gold, is the most important traded spice in the world, and the name comes from the Tamil word *pippali*.

The important thing about using spices is ensuring they're fresh. Whole spices keep longer than ground, which you should try to use within twelve months. Always keep them in airtight containers, rather than ripped-open bags, and away from heat and light.

When I was growing up, my grandmother Meenakshi never used fennel seeds in her cooking. Priests and Brahmins had less spices in their cooking, believing it aroused the senses, including lust, but my grandmother loved cloves, cardamom, cinnamon, nutmeg, and pepper. These spices created a lighter, simpler flavor to our family's food that influences my cooking to this day.

While I use fennel, I avoid creating complex masalas using thirty-six different spices, believing that it's better to taste the individual flavors of spices and the way they affect the food.

If you're not used to using spices, you may be nervous at first, but the instant you taste the dish you will wonder how you have lived your life without them; they are what's been missing without you realizing it … this was how I felt when I met my spice girl, Suba.

chicken chukka

chettiyar chicken

This Southern Indian dish packs a punch in flavor, with its robust spicing. It originates from the region of Chettinad, in a city called Karaikudi. The affluent Chettiyars often traveled to Myanmar (Burma) and other countries for timber trade and thus brought a variety of spices back to India; naturally the use of spices in Chettiyar cuisine is abundant. Originally, spices were used in India partly to disguise and improve poor ingredients, but now I use them to enhance flavors.

½ cup (4 fl oz/120 ml) vegetable or sunflower oil

2 red onions, sliced

1 tablespoon crushed garlic

2-inch (5-cm) piece of ginger, finely shredded

2 tomatoes, chopped

8 skinless chicken pieces (thigh, breast, and leg)

12 curry leaves

MASALA PASTE

2 tablespoons coriander seeds

3½ oz (100 g) shredded coconut

1 tablespoon cumin seeds

1 tablespoon black peppercorns

2 teaspoons fennel seeds

10 dried red chilies

6 whole cloves

4 fresh bay leaves

3 pieces of cassia bark (see glossary)

3 green cardamom pods

2 star anise

SERVES 4–6 AS PART OF A SHARED MEAL

To make the masala paste, heat a medium dry-frying pan over medium heat, add the coriander seeds and lightly toast for about 1 minute, shaking the pan regularly. Add the remaining ingredients and cook for 2 minutes or until fragrant and slightly colored, stirring regularly. This is done to release the flavors of the whole spices before grinding. Grind the spices in a spice grinder until finely ground. Add ¼–½ cup (2–4 fl oz/60–125 ml) of water and grind to a semi-smooth paste.

Heat ⅓ cup (2½ fl oz/80 ml) of the oil in a large heavy-based saucepan over medium heat, add the onion and cook for 6–8 minutes or until golden brown. Add the garlic and ginger (reserving some ginger to garnish) and cook for 1 minute. Stir in the tomato and cook for 2 minutes.

Add the masala paste and the chicken and stir gently to coat the chicken pieces.

Add ½ cup (4 fl oz/125 ml) of water and cook, covered, over low heat for 20 minutes or until the chicken is cooked.

While the chicken is cooking, heat the remaining oil in a frying pan over low heat and fry half of the curry leaves for 1–2 minutes or until just crisp. Set aside.

Once the chicken is cooked, add the remaining curry leaves and cook for 2 minutes. Remove from the heat and serve garnished with the ginger and fried curry leaves.

gutti venkai koora

stuffed eggplant

Gutti venkai koora literally translates to stuffed, eggplant, dry. It uses powerful, enigmatic spices, full of flavor and texture. This dish is loved by the staff (particularly our Andhra regiment!) at Abhi's.

12 baby eggplants

2 tablespoons tamarind pulp
(see glossary)

½ cup (4 fl oz/125 ml) vegetable
or sunflower oil

¼ teaspoon black mustard seeds

⅛ teaspoon fenugreek seeds

½ teaspoon split urad dal (black
lentils/black gram) (see glossary)

10 curry leaves

2 dried red chilies

finely shredded ginger, to garnish

FILLING

1 tablespoon vegetable oil

2 onions, thinly sliced

6 garlic cloves, finely chopped

3 dried red chilies

3 tablespoons raw peanuts

3 tablespoons shredded coconut

1 tablespoon coriander seeds

1 teaspoon cumin seeds

2 teaspoons chana dal (see glossary)

¼ teaspoon asafetida (see glossary)

¼ teaspoon white sesame seeds

10 curry leaves

SERVES 4–5 AS PART OF A SHARED MEAL

Slit each eggplant from the base into quarters, but do not slit all the way, just enough to make a space to put the filling inside. Sprinkle a bit of salt onto the cut eggplant and set aside.

To make the filling, heat the oil in a frying pan over medium heat, add the onion and garlic and cook for 6–8 minutes or until light brown. Set aside to cool.

Heat a small dry-frying pan over medium heat and lightly toast, one ingredient at a time, the chilies, peanuts, coconut, coriander seeds, cumin seeds, chana dal, asafetida, sesame seeds, and curry leaves. Toast each, shaking the pan regularly, until fragrant but not burnt. Add all of the toasted ingredients to the onion mixture.

Put the tamarind pulp in a small bowl. Add 1 cup (8 fl oz/ 250 ml) of water and combine. Set aside.

Fill the eggplant openings with the filling.

Heat 2 tablespoons of the oil in a large heavy-based frying pan over medium–high heat, add the eggplant and fry until lightly golden and seared on all sides. Remove from the pan.

Heat the remaining oil in the same pan over medium–high heat, add the mustard seeds and let them crackle for 20–30 seconds. Add the fenugreek, urad dal, curry leaves, and dried chilies and cook for 1 minute.

Put the filled eggplants carefully into the pan and cook, covered, for 7–8 minutes or until soft, shaking the pan occasionally. Be careful not to shake too hard, or you will break the eggplants.

When the eggplants are soft to the touch, remove the lid, stir in the tamarind mixture and cook, uncovered, for 7–10 minutes or until the sauce has reduced to a coating consistency. Garnish with the ginger and serve.

palak patta chaat

indian street snack

This famous roadside favorite is traditionally not a dish prepared in Indian homes. It's a dish best eaten outside in the middle of a shopping spree. The regular dish comprises wheat crisps covered in yogurt, and tamarind and coriander chutneys. I gave the dish a makeover at Abhi's with battered and fried spinach leaves replacing the humble wheat crisps. The tamarind chutney has the addition of sweet dates to balance its sourness.

FRIED SPINACH LEAVES

1¼ cups (5½ oz/150 g)
chickpea flour (besan)

1¾ oz (50 g) rice flour

½ teaspoon red chili powder

2 teaspoons salt

peanut or canola oil,
for deep-frying

1 bunch spinach, leaves picked,
washed and patted dry
(you will need about 20 leaves)

MINT & CORIANDER CHUTNEY

½ bunch mint, leaves picked

1 bunch cilantro (coriander),
roughly chopped

4 long green chilies, chopped

1 tablespoon lemon juice

2 teaspoons finely grated ginger

¼ teaspoon ground black pepper

1 teaspoon salt

DATE & TAMARIND CHUTNEY

1 oz (30 g) pitted dates, chopped

1 tablespoon tamarind concentrate
(see glossary)

1 tablespoon grated palm sugar (jaggery)

2½ teaspoons ground cumin

TOMATO CHILI CHUTNEY

2 ripe tomatoes

4 long red chilies, chopped

2½ teaspoons sweet paprika

YOGURT DRESSING

1 tablespoon ground cumin

1 cup (9¼ oz/260 g) Greek-style yogurt

1 tablespoon superfine sugar

TO SERVE

3½ oz (100 g) sebago potato, boiled
until tender, peeled, then diced

4½ oz (125 g) canned chickpeas,
rinsed and drained

2 teaspoons chopped cilantro (coriander)

To make the fried spinach leaves, first make the batter. Combine the flours, chili powder, and salt in a bowl. Make a well in the center, then gradually add 1¼ cup (10 fl oz/290 ml) of water and whisk until smooth. Cover and set aside until required.

To make the mint and coriander chutney, put all of the ingredients in a food processor and process until smooth. Transfer to a small bowl, cover, and set aside until required.

To make the date and tamarind chutney, combine all of the ingredients in a small saucepan, add ⅓ cup (2½ fl oz/80 ml) of water and cook over low heat for 10 minutes or until the dates have softened. Strain through a fine mesh sieve into a bowl, discarding the solids. Cool, then cover and set aside until required.

To make the tomato chili chutney, score a shallow cross in the base of the tomatoes. Put in a heatproof bowl and cover with boiling water. Leave for 30 seconds, then transfer to cold water and peel the skin away from the cross. Cut the tomatoes in half, scoop out the seeds with a teaspoon, and discard. Roughly dice the flesh, combine with the chili and paprika in a small saucepan over low heat and simmer for 10–

15 minutes or until soft. Strain the mixture through a fine mesh sieve, discarding the liquid. Cool, then cover and set aside until required.

To make the yogurt dressing, heat a small frying pan over medium–high heat, add the cumin, and dry-fry for about 30 seconds, shaking the pan regularly. Put the yogurt and sugar in a bowl, add the cumin, and stir to combine. Cover and refrigerate until required.

When you're ready to serve, fry the spinach leaves. To do this, heat about 4 inches (10 cm) of oil in a deep-fryer or large saucepan to 355°F (180°C) or until a cube of bread turns golden brown in 15 seconds. Dip the spinach leaves, one at a time, into the batter, shaking off any excess, and deep-fry, in batches, until crisp and golden. Remove with a slotted spoon and drain on a paper towel.

To serve, divide the fried spinach leaves among plates, scatter with the potato and chickpeas, spoon over a little yogurt dressing, then top with 1 teaspoon of each of the chutneys. Sprinkle with the cilantro and serve immediately.

mysore kozhi

mysore chili chicken

2 lb 4 oz (1 kg) boneless, skinless chicken thigh fillets, each cut into thirds

½ cup (4½ oz/130 g) plain thick yogurt

3½ oz (100 g) grated coconut (see glossary)

⅓ cup (2½ fl oz/80 ml) vegetable or sunflower oil

6 green cardamom pods

1-inch (2.5-cm) piece of cinnamon stick

6 whole cloves

1 onion, sliced

1 tablespoon finely grated ginger

1 tablespoon crushed garlic

2 teaspoons ground turmeric

1 tablespoon Kashmiri chili powder (see glossary)

1 tomato, chopped

4 small green chilies, halved lengthwise

½ cup (3½ fl oz/100 ml) coconut milk

finely shredded ginger and finely chopped cilantro (coriander), to garnish (optional)

SERVES 4–6 AS PART OF A SHARED MEAL

Combine the chicken and yogurt and leave to marinate for 20 minutes.

Put half of the coconut in a spice grinder with ½ cup (4 fl oz/ 125 ml) of water and blend to a fine paste—it's very important that it is a fine paste. Remove from the spice grinder and set aside. Repeat with the remaining coconut and another ½ cup (4 fl oz/ 125 ml) of water. Set aside.

Heat the oil in a heavy-based saucepan over medium heat, add the cardamom, cinnamon stick, and cloves, and cook for about 1 minute or until fragrant. Add the onion and cook for 6–8 minutes or until golden brown. Add the ginger and garlic and cook for 1 minute. Add the turmeric and chili powder, tomato and green chili and cook for 2 minutes.

Add the ground coconut paste with 1 cup (8 fl oz/250 ml) of water and cook, covered, for 15 minutes.

Add the chicken and cook, covered, for 15 minutes.

Stir in the coconut milk and cook for 5 minutes or until the chicken is cooked and tender. Garnish with the ginger and cilantro to serve.

aki's railway goat curry

Our goat curry has survived the many menu changes over the years. In India, mutton refers to goat meat (not sheep as it does in Australia). This dish is cooked on the bone to deliver succulent pieces of goat in a rich sauce. It was originally a travelers' meal on the Southern Indian railways. It's said that the dish was created when a train hit a goat on the tracks… Bingo, goat curry! We have modified it, replacing the more traditional coconut oil, and added our unique spicing.

½ cup (3½ fl oz / 100 ml) sunflower oil

3 dried bay leaves

1-inch (2.5-cm) piece of cinnamon stick

6 green cardamom pods

9 whole cloves

2 red onions, thinly sliced

2 teaspoons crushed garlic

1½ tablespoons finely grated ginger

½ teaspoon ground turmeric

1 teaspoon red chili powder

1 tablespoon ground coriander

3 tomatoes, chopped

3 lb 5 oz (1.5 kg) goat leg, bone in, cut into ¾-inch (2-cm) cubes (ask your butcher to do this)

4 cilantro (coriander) sprigs, plus whole leaves to garnish

pinch of mace threads or ground mace

SERVES 8–10 AS PART OF A SHARED MEAL

Heat the oil in a casserole dish over medium–low heat, add the bay leaves, cinnamon stick, cardamom, and cloves, and cook until fragrant. Add the onion and cook for 8–10 minutes or until golden brown. Add the garlic and cook for 1 minute. Add the ginger, turmeric, chili powder, and ground coriander and cook for 2 minutes, adding 1 tablespoon of water to stop the ground spices from burning.

Add the tomato and cook until you see some oil separation around the edges.

Add the goat, season with salt, stir to coat the meat with the mixture, and continue to stir regularly for 5 minutes or until the meat releases its juices.

Add 4 cups (35 fl oz / 1 liter) of water, bring to a boil, then cook, covered, for 1½ hours. Check the consistency of the sauce. It should not be too thin; if it is, cook, uncovered, for 20–30 minutes. Add the whole sprigs of cilantro and the mace, and remove from the heat. Garnish with the cilantro leaves.

Tip: Slow cooking will ensure tender meat.

masala lamb cutlets

You should ask my next-door butcher about this dish. He has been my meat supplier from day one for both restaurants. The secret to this dish is the quality of the lamb; his is from Junee in the Riverina region in New South Wales. When the meat is this good, it doesn't need much treatment.

1 teaspoon ground mace

1 teaspoon ground cardamom

2 teaspoons fennel seeds

¾-inch (2-cm) piece of ginger, roughly chopped

3 garlic cloves, bruised

½ bunch cilantro (coriander), leaves and stalks

3 tablespoons lime juice

1 teaspoon Kashmiri chili powder (see glossary)

½ teaspoon ground turmeric

12 French-trimmed lamb cutlets

¼ teaspoon saffron threads

3 tablespoons plain thick yogurt

1 tablespoon olive oil

SERVES 6 AS PART OF A SHARED MEAL

Combine the mace, cardamom, and fennel in a bowl to make a garam masala and set aside.

Using a mortar and pestle or small spice grinder, grind the ginger, garlic, and a pinch of salt to a paste. Add the cilantro leaves and stalks, and grind to a paste. Transfer to a large bowl.

Add the garam masala, lime juice, chili powder, turmeric, and ½ teaspoon of salt to the bowl and combine. Add the lamb and toss to coat well, then cover and marinate in the fridge for 2 hours.

Put the saffron threads in a small bowl with 2 tablespoons (1 fl oz/30 ml) of boiling water. Cool, then add the yogurt, season with a little salt, and stir until smooth. Add to the lamb and coat well.

Preheat the oven to 350°F (180°C/Gas 4) and line a baking tray with parchment paper.

Heat the oil in a large frying pan over medium–high heat, add the lamb in batches, and cook for 1 minute each side to sear. Transfer to the prepared tray and roast for 5–7 minutes for medium or until cooked to your liking. Rest for 4 minutes before serving.

goan pork sausage curry

I first encountered this curry many years ago at my friend Noel Rodriguez's house. He is from Goa, once a Portuguese colony, and the Goan sausage traditionally used in this dish is a relative of the Portuguese chorizo, only much spicier, as it has been adapted and made with the spices available in India. The potatoes act as an excellent foil to the heat of the chili in the dish.

3 tablespoons vegetable or sunflower oil

½ teaspoon cumin seeds

1 large onion, sliced

1 tablespoon finely grated ginger

2 teaspoons crushed garlic

½ teaspoon ground turmeric

1 teaspoon ground cumin

1 teaspoon red chili powder

2 teaspoons ground coriander

1 tomato, diced

1 tablespoon malt vinegar

4 new (baby) potatoes, skin on, cut into ¾-inch (2-cm) slices

1 lb 5 oz (600 g) spicy fresh pork sausage (such as chorizo), casings removed and meat cut into ¾-inch (2-cm) slices

finely chopped cilantro (coriander), to garnish

Heat the oil in a heavy-based frying pan over medium heat, add the cumin seeds, and cook for 1 minute.

Add the onion and cook over medium–low heat for about 5 minutes or until softened and translucent, but do not brown.

Add the ginger and garlic and cook for 1 minute.

Add the turmeric, cumin, chili powder, ground coriander, and tomato and cook for 5–7 minutes, adding 1–2 tablespoons of water to prevent the spices from sticking to the base of the pan.

Add 1½ cups (13 fl oz/375 ml) of water, the vinegar, potatoes, and sausage and cook for 10–15 minutes or until the potatoes and sausage are cooked. Check the seasoning and garnish with the cilantro to serve.

duck mappas

keralan duck curry

This is a very popular dish at Aki's. It's rich in flavor, light in consistency, and sweet from the flavor of the coconut and French shallots. Not much additional oil is required to cook this dish as the duck breasts cook in their own fat. Duck is not the most popular meat in India, but the Keralites relish this dish.

6 duck breasts with skin and wing bone (see tip)

2 teaspoons red chili powder

2 teaspoons finely grated ginger

3½ tablespoons (1½ fl oz/50 ml) coconut oil

4 green cardamom pods

6 whole cloves

1 cinnamon stick

2 long green chilies, thinly sliced diagonally

2 sprigs of curry leaves

12 French shallots (eschalots), chopped

2-inch (5-cm) piece of ginger, finely shredded

1 cup (8 fl oz/250 ml) coconut milk

⅓ cup (2½ fl oz/80 ml) coconut cream

appams or iddiappams (see page 184), to serve

SERVES 6 AS PART OF A SHARED MEAL

Preheat the oven to 315°F (160°C/Gas 2–3) and put a baking dish in the oven to heat up.

Score the duck skin a few times with a knife, then rub the skin and meat with the chili powder, ginger, and a little salt. Put in the fridge to marinate for 30 minutes.

Heat a large heavy-based frying pan over high heat, add 1 tablespoon of the coconut oil, and cook the duck in two batches, skin side down, for about 3 minutes or until seared. Turn over and sear the other side. This is just to seal the meat—do not overcook. Transfer the duck to the preheated baking dish and roast for 20 minutes. Remove the duck and set aside. Drain the excess fat from the baking dish but reserve the juices and set aside for adding to the sauce later.

Heat the remaining coconut oil in a large frying pan over medium–high heat. Add the cardamom, cloves, cinnamon, green chili, and curry leaves and let these splutter for a few seconds. Reduce the heat to low, add the shallot, and cook for 5 minutes or until softened, but without browning.

Add the ginger, coconut milk, reserved duck juices, and ½ cup (4 fl oz/125 ml) of water. Add the duck breasts and cook, covered, over low heat for 15 minutes or until the duck is almost cooked.

Add the coconut cream and cook, uncovered, for 5 minutes. Remove the duck from the pan and thickly slice, then return to the sauce. Serve with appams or iddiappams.

Tip: If you can't find duck breasts with the wing bone attached, simply use duck breasts. Roasting the duck slowly at a low heat will keep them juicy and tender.

tandoori chooza

tandoori spatchcock

2 lb 4 oz (1 kg) spatchcock (baby chicken), butterflied

½ teaspoon ground turmeric

1 teaspoon red chili powder

1 tablespoon finely grated ginger

2 teaspoons crushed garlic

3 tablespoons malt vinegar

3 tablespoons Greek-style yogurt

3 tablespoons mustard oil (see glossary)

2 tablespoons melted butter or ghee (see glossary)

mint and yogurt sauce (see page 212), to serve

GARAM MASALA

1 teaspoon grated nutmeg

1 teaspoon ground mace

½ teaspoon ground cardamom

½ teaspoon ground cloves

½ teaspoon ground star anise

2 teaspoons ground cumin

SERVES 2–3 AS PART OF A SHARED MEAL

Remove the skin from the spatchcock and score each breast. Combine the turmeric, chili powder, ginger, garlic, vinegar, and ½ teaspoon of salt in a bowl and rub over the spatchcock to coat well. Put in the fridge to marinate for at least 3 hours.

Combine all of the garam masala ingredients in a small bowl.

Put the yogurt in a bowl and beat until smooth, then add the garam masala, a touch of salt, and the mustard oil, and stir to combine. Rub all over the spatchcock. Put in the fridge to marinate for another 3 hours.

Remove the spatchcock from the fridge 20 minutes before cooking to bring to room temperature.

Preheat a barbecue or grill (broiler) to hot. Thread two long metal skewers through the spatchcock crosswise to make it easier to handle. Cook on the barbecue with the breast facing the heat for 6 minutes or until cooked through, or under the grill for 10–12 minutes. Ensure both the thigh and breast meat are cooked by testing with a metal skewer—the juices should run clear with no traces of pink.

Remove the spatchcock and let it rest for 5 minutes. Cut into pieces, brush with the melted butter or ghee, and serve with the mint and yogurt sauce.

fried masala fish

1 lb 2 oz–1 lb 5 oz (500–600 g) whole snapper, cleaned, gutted, and scaled (see tip)

juice of 2 limes

3 tablespoons fine rice flour

2 tablespoons vegetable oil

fried curry leaves, to garnish

black salt, to garnish (optional)

MASALA PASTE

2 tablespoons Kashmiri chili powder (see glossary)

2 teaspoons sweet paprika

2 teaspoons ground cumin

1 teaspoon ground black pepper

½ teaspoon ground turmeric

1 tablespoon finely grated ginger

2 teaspoons crushed garlic

½ cup (3½ fl oz/100 ml) gingili (unscented sesame oil) (see glossary)

SERVES 2 AS PART OF A SHARED MEAL

Preheat the oven to 325°F (170°C/Gas 3).

Wash the fish thoroughly in water to get rid of any excess scales. Score the fish diagonally on both sides to form a checkered pattern, so the masala can seep inside the fish. Pour the lime juice over the fish and set aside for 10 minutes.

Combine all of the masala paste ingredients in a bowl to form a smooth paste (do not add any water).

Coat the fish all over with the masala paste, then dust the fish in the rice flour.

Heat the oil in a heavy-based ovenproof frying pan over medium–low heat (see tip), add the fish, and cook for 2 minutes each side to sear.

Transfer the pan to the oven and bake for 8 minutes or until the fish is just cooked through. Cut into large pieces to serve.

Serve garnished with the fried curry leaves and black salt.

Tip: Traditionally the fish used in this recipe is pomfret, which is occasionally available from select fishmongers. Whole silver dory or fillets of ocean perch or blue-eye trevalla are also good in this dish.

Cooking on high heat will burn the rice flour and the chili powder.

kori gazi

mangalore chicken curry

Mrs. Shetty of Mangalore, a family friend, visited us in Sydney and enjoyed my cooking. In return she shared her family secret to this dish. The effort of roasting spices individually for this dish makes all the difference. Many commercial versions of this dish are available, but this is her home-style treasure.

1½ tablespoons coriander seeds

½ teaspoon black peppercorns

¼ teaspoon fenugreek seeds

1 teaspoon cumin seeds

¼ teaspoon chili flakes

3½ oz (100 g) shredded coconut

¼ teaspoon ground turmeric

⅓ cup (2½ fl oz/80 ml) vegetable or sunflower oil

10 garlic cloves, sliced

3 onions, sliced

2 tablespoons tamarind pulp (see glossary)

⅓ cup (2½ fl oz/80 ml) coconut milk

2 lb 4 oz (1 kg) boneless, skinless chicken thigh fillets, diced

2 tablespoons (1 oz/30 g) ghee (see glossary)

10 curry leaves

Heat a dry-frying pan over medium heat, add the coriander seeds, and cook, stirring regularly until lightly toasted and aromatic. Remove from the pan and set aside. Repeat separately with the black peppercorns, fenugreek seeds, cumin seeds, and chili flakes.

In the same pan, toast the coconut to a light golden color. Transfer the coconut to a spice grinder with the toasted spices, turmeric, and ½–1 cup (4–8 fl oz/125–250 ml) of water and grind to a fine paste—you will need to do this in several batches to ensure it is fine, which is important.

Heat the oil in a heavy-based saucepan over medium heat, add the garlic (reserving 1 teaspoon for finishing) and cook for 1 minute. Add the onion and cook for 10 minutes or until golden brown.

Stir in the coconut and spice paste, tamarind pulp, and coconut milk. Add the chicken and cook, covered, over low heat for 20–25 minutes, stirring occasionally.

To finish, heat the ghee in a small frying pan over low heat, add the reserved garlic and the curry leaves, and cook for 30 seconds, then pour the mixture over the chicken. Check the seasoning and serve immediately.

tabak maaz

crispy milk-poached lamb ribs

On one of my visits to Delhi, I got to taste this fabulous Kashmiri preparation at a place called Ahad Sons. It is a simple takeaway shop, which serves some of the most amazing Kashmiri food in Delhi. Kashmiri cuisine has been relatively unexplored in mainstream Indian cooking, but it offers some very rich, flavorsome dishes involving some great cooking techniques and unusual ingredients. Tabak maaz is a speciality served at festive Wazwan banquets.

2 cups (17 fl oz/500 ml) milk

12 lamb ribs, cut into 3-rib pieces

1 teaspoon aniseed

2 teaspoons ground ginger

½ teaspoon ground turmeric

6 whole cloves

2 dried bay leaves

½ teaspoon black cumin seeds
(see glossary)

2 black cardamom pods

ghee, for shallow-frying
(see glossary)

½ teaspoon amchur (dry mango
powder) (see glossary)

½ teaspoon Kashmiri chili
powder (see glossary)

¼ teaspoon garam masala
(see page 125)

store-bought Indian pickled onions
and parathas (see glossary),
to serve

SERVES 4–6 AS A SNACK OR STARTER

Put the milk, lamb, aniseed, ginger, turmeric, cloves, bay leaves, cumin, and cardamom in a heavy-based saucepan and bring to a boil, then reduce the heat to a simmer and cook, uncovered, for about 20 minutes or until the milk evaporates and the meat is tender, ensuring the base of the pan does not burn. Add ½ cup (4 fl oz/125 ml) of water during the cooking, if required.

Allow the lamb to cool to room temperature, and scrape off any whole spices sticking to the meat.

Heat some ghee in a large deep-sided frying pan over medium heat, add the lamb, and shallow-fry until crisp all over. The aim is to get a crisp exterior while the meat remains tender and juicy inside.

Combine the amchur, chili powder, and garam masala and sprinkle over the ribs. Serve hot with pickled onions and parathas.

arikadukka

steamed stuffed mussels

I ate these green lip mussels in Thalassery (Tellicherry), a coastal town in the north of Kerala. I was intrigued by this fascinating technique of first steaming and then frying the mussels.

¾ cup (6½ oz/180 g) grated coconut (see glossary)

¾ teaspoon cumin seeds

¾ teaspoon aniseed

2 green cardamom pods

1½ cups (12¾ oz/360 g) white iddiappam flour (see glossary)

vegetable or sunflower oil, for shallow-frying

9 French shallots (eschalots), chopped

25 green lip mussels

½ teaspoon garam masala (see page 125)

½ teaspoon red chili powder

fried curry leaves, to garnish

Put the coconut, cumin seeds, aniseed, and cardamom in a spice grinder and grind to a fine paste.

Put 1½ cups (13 fl oz/375 ml) of water in a saucepan, bring to a boil, then add the iddiappam flour and stir until it is a thick dough. Add the coconut mixture and cook for 2 minutes. Remove from the heat and set aside to cool. This should feel like a soft, gnocchi-like dough.

Heat 1 tablespoon of oil in a small frying pan over medium heat, add the shallots and cook until light brown. Drain on a paper towel to remove any excess oil, then add to the dough. Set aside.

Scrub the mussels and pull out the hairy beards. Discard any that are broken. If there are any open ones, give them a tap on the counter and if they do not close, discard them. Lightly steam the mussels in a saucepan with about 2 inches (5 cm) of boiling water, until they just open. Drain and when cool enough to handle, carefully pry open the mussels, using the edge of a butter knife, making sure the two shells remain attached. Carefully remove the mussel meat, reserving the shells. Wrap each mussel with some of the dough, return to the shells, and clean off any excess dough hanging outside the shells.

Line a metal or bamboo steamer basket with baking paper to prevent sticking. Put the mussels in a single layer in the basket, cover with a tight-fitting lid and steam over a saucepan or wok of simmering water for 20 minutes. Remove from the heat and allow to cool. Once the mussels cool down, the dough will have set over the mussel meat. Remove the dough-encased mussels from the shells.

Heat the oil in a deep-sided frying pan over medium–high heat, add the mussels and shallow-fry until golden brown all over. Remove from the pan, drain on a paper towel and sprinkle over the garam masala and chili powder, then garnish with curry leaves.

scampi ajadhina

pan-grilled scampi

8 scampi, unshelled

1 teaspoon ground turmeric

juice of 1 lime

3 tablespoons vegetable or sunflower oil

a few drops of curry leaf–infused oil (see page 188)

SPICE POWDER

½ cup (1½ oz/45 g) shredded coconut

2 garlic cloves, roughly chopped

2 dried red chilies

2 teaspoons Kashmiri chili powder (see glossary)

2 teaspoons coriander seeds

½ teaspoon carom seeds (ajwain) (see glossary)

¼ teaspoon cumin seeds

¼ teaspoon ground turmeric

2 teaspoons tamarind pulp (see glossary)

Preheat the oven to 350°F (180°C/Gas 4).

To make the spice powder, heat a dry-frying pan over medium–high heat, add all of the ingredients except the tamarind, and lightly toast for about 1 minute, shaking the pan regularly. Transfer to a spice grinder with the tamarind pulp, season with salt, and coarsely grind (see tip).

To prepare the scampi, snip off any very long legs using a sharp knife. Carefully butterfly each scampi, slicing through the back shell, and remove the intestinal vein. Rub the scampi with the turmeric and 2 teaspoons of the lime juice.

Heat 2 tablespoons of the vegetable oil in an ovenproof frying pan, add the scampi, flesh side down, and cook for 30 seconds to lightly sear.

Turn over the scampi, drizzle over the remaining oil, sprinkle with about half of the spice powder, and immediately put the pan in the oven and roast for 5–7 minutes.

Drizzle with the curry leaf–infused oil and remaining lime juice and serve hot.

Tip: You can store the spice powder in an airtight jar in the fridge for up to 1 week. Use the remaining spice powder as a rub for fish.

tok jhol

sour fish curry

1 teaspoon ground turmeric

1 tablespoon vegetable or sunflower oil

14 oz (400 g) garfish, bone from head removed (ask your fishmonger to do this), cut into bite-sized pieces

4 small green chilies, roughly chopped

3 tablespoons tamarind pulp (see glossary)

½ teaspoon grated palm sugar (jaggery) or soft brown sugar

TEMPERING

2 teaspoons mustard oil (see glossary)

2 teaspoons panch phoran masala (see glossary)

1½ tablespoons chickpea flour (besan)

SERVES 3–4 AS PART OF A SHARED MEAL

Combine ½ teaspoon of salt with ½ teaspoon of the turmeric and 1 teaspoon of the oil. Rub all over the fish and set aside for 30 minutes.

Put the chili in a small blender or spice grinder and grind to a coarse paste.

To make the tempering, heat the mustard oil in a small frying pan over high heat until just smoking, add the panch phoran masala and allow it to crackle. Add the chickpea flour and cook for 10 seconds. Remove from the heat and set aside.

Combine 1 teaspoon of the oil, the remaining turmeric, the tamarind pulp, palm sugar, the green chili paste, and a pinch of salt in a large bowl. Add the fish and the tempering and mix well.

Heat the remaining oil in a frying pan over medium heat. Add the fish mixture and ½ cup (4 fl oz/125 ml) of water and cook, covered, for about 5 minutes or until the fish is cooked, adding a little extra water if necessary. The sauce should be like a thick gravy. If it is a little thin, remove the fish from the pan, then cook the sauce, uncovered, for 1–2 minutes to thicken. Check the seasoning and serve.

nalli gosht patiala

lamb shanks patiala

6 tablespoons (3 fl oz/90 ml) vegetable or sunflower oil

3 black cardamom pods

6 green cardamom pods

1-inch (2.5-cm) piece of cinnamon stick

1 teaspoon black cumin seeds

8 whole cloves

2 onions, sliced

1 tablespoon finely grated ginger

1 tablespoon crushed garlic

½ teaspoon ground turmeric

2 teaspoons red chili powder

1½ tablespoons ground coriander

4–6 lamb shanks, cut into ¾-inch (2-cm) rounds (ask your butcher to do this)

½ cup (4½ oz/125 g) tomato paste (concentrated purée)

¼ teaspoon ground mace

¼ teaspoon grated nutmeg

2 tablespoons roughly chopped cilantro (coriander)

parathas or rotis, to serve (see glossary)

SERVES 6 AS PART OF A SHARED MEAL

Heat the oil in a large heavy-based casserole dish over medium–high heat, add the cardamom, cinnamon stick, cumin, and cloves and cook for 1–2 minutes or until fragrant. Add the onion and cook for 5 minutes or until golden. Stir in the ginger and garlic and cook for 2 minutes, sprinkling with 1 tablespoon of water, if necessary, to prevent it from burning. Add the turmeric, chili powder, and ground coriander and cook for 2 minutes.

Add the lamb, stir to coat in the spices and cook for 2 minutes or until seared on all sides.

Add the tomato paste and 4 cups (35 fl oz/1 liter) of water and cook, covered, over low heat for 1–1½ hours, adding extra water if the sauce evaporates too quickly. The meat should be almost falling off the bone. Stir in the mace and nutmeg, season with salt, and remove from the heat. Garnish with the chopped cilantro and serve with hot parathas or rotis.

nandu milagu masala

coconut chili crab

2 lb 4 oz (1 kg) live blue swimmer crab

2 tablespoons vegetable or sunflower oil

1 large onion, sliced

2 dried Kashmiri chilies (see glossary)

2 teaspoons finely grated ginger

2 teaspoons crushed garlic

1 tomato, chopped

3 tablespoons coconut cream

curry leaves, to garnish (optional)

MASALA PASTE

5½ oz (150 g) grated coconut or shredded coconut (see glossary)

6 dried Kashmiri chilies (see glossary) or 1½ tablespoons hot paprika

1 teaspoon black peppercorns

1 tablespoon coriander seeds

2 teaspoons cumin seeds

1 teaspoon ground turmeric

SERVES 4 AS PART OF A SHARED MEAL

Carefully place the crab in the freezer for 1 hour to put it to sleep. To prepare the crab, pull off the top shell and set aside. Remove and discard the feathery gills on either side. Using a meat cleaver or large knife, cut the crab into quarters with legs attached. Cut off each claw. Lightly crush the shell of the claws and legs with the back of the knife.

To make the masala paste, put all of the ingredients in a spice grinder and process until fine. Remove half from the grinder and set aside. Add 3 tablespoons of water to the grinder and blend to form a very smooth, fine paste. Remove from the grinder and set aside. Repeat with the remaining ground spices.

Heat the oil in a large heavy-based saucepan over medium heat, add the onion and chilies, and cook for about 5 minutes. Add the ginger and garlic and cook for 2 minutes. Add the masala paste and cook for 2 minutes.

Add 2 cups (17 fl oz/500 ml) of water and the tomato and simmer over low heat for 15 minutes, adding the coconut cream towards the end of the cooking time.

Add the crab claws and cook for 5 minutes, then add the remaining crab pieces, adding a little more water, if necessary. Cook, covered, for about 3 minutes or until the crab is cooked through. Scatter over the curry leaves to garnish.

kakori kebabs

minced lamb kebabs

The opulence of the royals' day starts with rich kebabs. They are meant to give them energy for the day. The meat is passed through a meat grinder a couple of times to make a fine paste, so the texture of the cooked kebab is almost like pâté. Due to the high fat content of the ground meat, it needs to set and chill in the fridge before you can mold it onto the skewers and cook it.

3 tablespoons chickpea flour (besan)

1 teaspoon yellow chili powder (see glossary)

½ teaspoon ground mace

1 teaspoon ground cardamom

½ teaspoon ground white pepper

2 lb 4 oz (1 kg) finely ground lamb (passed through a meat grinder twice—ask your butcher to do this)

1¼ cup (9½ oz/270 g) ghee (see glossary)

1½ tablespoons finely grated ginger

1 tablespoon crushed garlic

1 teaspoon garam masala (see page 125)

green chutney (see page 210), to serve

MAKES 10–12 / SERVES 5–6 AS PART OF A SHARED MEAL

Heat a small dry-frying pan over medium–high heat, add the chickpea flour and lightly toast, shaking the pan regularly. Combine with the chili powder, mace, cardamom, and pepper and set aside.

Combine the lamb with the ghee, ginger, garlic, and garam masala in a large bowl and knead to a doughy consistency. As you knead, the color of the meat will become paler and lighter. Add the chickpea flour mixture and knead to combine well. Put in the fridge for 1 hour to firm up.

Divide the mixture into 10–12 portions and, with slightly wet hands, mold the mixture onto metal skewers.

Preheat a charcoal barbecue or regular barbecue grill plate to medium heat. Cook the skewers for 8–10 minutes or until browned and cooked through—the cooking time will depend on how close the kebabs are to the heat. Serve with the chutney.

seafood panch phoran

five-spice seafood curry

2 lb 4 oz (1 kg) ripe roma (plum) tomatoes

2 tablespoons sunflower oil

6 dried red chilies

1 teaspoon panch phoran masala (see glossary)

1 red onion, diced

½ teaspoon red chili powder

1 tablespoon finely grated ginger

2 lb 4 oz (1 kg) mixed seafood, such as scallops, shrimp, white fish pieces, and calamari

6 cilantro (coriander) sprigs, leaves roughly chopped

1 tablespoon finely shredded ginger

SERVES 6–8 AS PART OF A SHARED MEAL

Score a shallow cross in the base of the tomatoes. Put in a heatproof bowl and cover with boiling water. Leave for 30 seconds, then transfer to cold water and peel the skin away from the cross. Cut the tomatoes in half, scoop out the seeds with a teaspoon and discard. Roughly chop the flesh and set aside.

Heat the oil in a frying pan over medium–high heat, add the dried chilies and cook until the tips of the chilies turn black. Add the panch phoran masala and cook for 1–2 minutes.

Add the onion and cook over medium–low heat for 5 minutes or until soft and translucent, but without browning. Add the chili powder, ginger, and tomato and cook for 15 minutes.

Add the seafood, increase the heat to medium, and cook for 3 minutes or until the seafood is cooked. Serve garnished with the cilantro and ginger.

Tip: The sweetness of the seafood is enhanced with the sweetness of the tomato, while the panch phoran masala gives the dish its balance.

whole snapper recheado

spice-crusted whole snapper

2 small snapper, cleaned, gutted, and scaled

3 tablespoons vegetable or sunflower oil

thinly sliced red onion, to garnish

fried onions, to garnish

MASALA PASTE

6 dried Kashmiri chilies (see glossary)

1 onion, roughly chopped

6 garlic cloves, roughly chopped

2-inch (5-cm) piece of ginger, roughly chopped

10 black peppercorns

4 whole cloves

1-inch (2.5-cm) piece of cassia bark (see glossary)

½ teaspoon cumin seeds

¼ teaspoon ground turmeric

⅓ cup (2½ fl oz/80 ml) toddy vinegar (see glossary), malt vinegar, or palm vinegar (see glossary)

SERVES 4–6 AS PART OF A SHARED MEAL

Preheat the oven to 350°F (180°C/Gas 4).

To make the masala paste, put all of the ingredients in a blender, season with salt, and blend to a smooth paste.

Wash the fish thoroughly in water to get rid of any excess scales. Score the fish with three diagonal cuts on both sides, so the masala can seep inside the fish. Rub the masala paste all over the fish.

Heat the oil in a large ovenproof frying pan over medium–high heat, add the fish, and cook briefly on both sides to sear. Cover with foil (to prevent the masala crust from burning), put the pan in the oven and roast for 5 minutes, then remove the foil and roast for another 5–10 minutes or until the fish is just cooked.

Garnish with the sliced red and fried onion, and drizzle over some of the pan juices to serve.

jhinge aloo posto

ridge gourd & potato

My head chef at Abhi's, Ranjan Choudhury, served us this beautiful dish for a lunch at his house. Even though it was specially prepared for Suba, being a vegetarian, I, the carnivore, couldn't keep my hands off it and Suba's plate too! Posto refers to white poppy seeds, which is a prominent ingredient in Bengali cooking.

¾ cup (3½ oz/100 g) white poppy seeds (see glossary)

3–4 small green chilies, chopped

1 lb 2 oz (500 g) ridge gourd (loofah)

⅓ cup (2½ fl oz/80 ml) vegetable or sunflower oil

½ teaspoon nigella seeds (onion seeds/kalonji) (see glossary)

1 onion, sliced

2 waxy potatoes, cut into 1¼-inch (3-cm) cubes

¼ teaspoon ground turmeric

SERVES 6 AS PART OF A SHARED MEAL

Soak the poppy seeds in 3 tablespoons of water for 20 minutes. Put the seeds and soaking water in a small blender with two-thirds of the chili and process to a fine paste.

Peel the ridges off the ridge gourd, removing the tough green outer layer to get a smooth surface. Halve the gourd lengthwise, then slice fairly thickly into half moons. Set aside.

Heat the oil in a medium saucepan over medium heat, add the nigella seeds, and cook for 30 seconds, then add the onion and cook for 3 minutes.

Add the potato, turmeric, remaining green chili, and the poppy seed paste, sprinkle with 1 tablespoon of water, and cook until the potato is well coated with the poppy seed paste. Stir in ⅓ cup (2½ fl oz/80 ml) of water and cook, covered, for 8 minutes, stirring regularly or until the potato is half cooked.

Add the ridge gourd and cook for 5–7 minutes, stirring regularly. Season with salt and serve hot.

chicken chettiyar milagu

tomato & pepper chicken curry

A delicious Chettinad dish, where tomatoes and pepper play dominant roles, without the use of coconut. This dish is cooked best by my youngest chef, Vikram Arumugam, who is a Chettiyar boy, and has been an integral part of Aki's since we opened.

3 tablespoons vegetable
or sunflower oil

1 teaspoon black mustard seeds

2 dried red chilies

¼ teaspoon fenugreek seeds

½ teaspoon cumin seeds

1 cinnamon stick

2 green cardamom pods

4 whole cloves

¼ teaspoon fennel seeds

1 onion, thinly sliced

1½ tablespoons finely grated
ginger

1½ tablespoons crushed garlic

1½ teaspoons ground turmeric

1 tablespoon red chili powder

2½ tablespoons ground coriander

7 oz (200 g) tomatoes, diced

4 small green chilies, halved
lengthwise

2 lb 4 oz (1 kg) chicken thigh fillets,
each cut into thirds

2 teaspoons cracked
black pepper

10 curry leaves

SERVES 6 AS PART OF A SHARED MEAL

Heat the oil in a large heavy-based saucepan over medium heat, add the mustard seeds and let them crackle for about 20 seconds. Add the red chilies, fenugreek, and cumin and cook for 1 minute. Add the cinnamon, cardamom, cloves, and fennel and cook for 1 minute.

Add the onion and cook for 6–8 minutes, stirring occasionally until almost golden brown. Add the ginger, garlic, and 1 teaspoon of water and cook for 1 minute.

Add the turmeric, chili powder, and ground coriander and cook for 2 minutes, sprinkling with 1–2 tablespoons of water to prevent the mixture from burning.

Add the tomato, green chili, and chicken and cook for 5 minutes or until the juices start to release from the chicken.

Add 1½ cups (12 fl oz/375 ml) of water and cook, covered, over low heat, for about 20 minutes or until the chicken is cooked through. Season with salt if necessary, then finish with the pepper and curry leaves.

Tip: Cilantro leaves aren't normally added to this dish, as they are too strong.

fish tikka

grilled swordfish

2 teaspoons finely grated ginger

2 teaspoons crushed garlic

¼ teaspoon ground turmeric

½ teaspoon red chili powder

2 tablespoons malt vinegar

¼ teaspoon garam masala (see page 125)

2 tablespoons chana dal (see glossary), toasted and finely ground, or toasted chickpea flour (besan)

⅛ teaspoon carom seeds (ajwain) (see glossary)

2 tablespoons mustard oil (see glossary)

1 lb 5 oz (600 g) swordfish steaks, cut into 6 portions

vegetable or sunflower oil, for brushing

green chutney (see page 210), to serve

SERVES 6 AS PART OF A SHARED MEAL

Combine all of the ingredients except the fish, oil, and chutney. Rub all over the fish and set aside to marinate for 30 minutes.

Preheat a barbecue grill plate or hotplate. Lightly brush with oil and grill the fish for 2 minutes on one side, then turn over and cook the other side for 2 minutes or until just cooked through. Serve with the green chutney.

sweet

A HAPPY FAMILY IS A SWEET BALANCE. Our boys, Abhi and Aki, who our restaurants are named after, are the ultimate "sweet" for us. Our desire for the restaurants to be successful has meant that our family spends a lot of time there. If you ask either Abhi or Aki, "What is family time?" I am sure they will answer, "The restaurant Abhi's." For all the missed homework, soccer goals, and dinnertime conversations, rather than resent the hours that the business took away from family time, Abhi and Aki have come to love the restaurants and are involved in day-to-day operations. We could not have asked for a sweeter ending.

In India, every happy moment is celebrated by sharing sweets. At festive occasions, weddings, and religious ceremonies, sweets are often served before any other foods. Indians believe, poetically, that by starting a meal sweetly life will also continue that way. In a Southern Indian wedding, for example, food is served on banana leaves and strict rules govern where food is put. Sweet things are always on the right-hand side, roughly at the four o'clock, which is where you start eating the meal in a counterclockwise direction. It's the same for thali plates across India—you always eat the sweet first.

When I met my wife, Suba, for the first time, it was over sweets. It's traditional for the bride's family to serve kesari (semolina cake), and Suba's mother made pineapple kesari (see page 205 for a recipe) that I loved so much I asked for seconds.

India even has its own version of the ice cream man to excite children: the kulfiwalla, who pushes his cart filled with kulfis, which come in a long conical shape with a popsicle stick.

Others sweets, such as halwa, are ubiquitous, yet differ between regions. In Mumbai (Bombay), the halwa is hard and caramelly and cut into cubes, while in the south it's softer and needs to be scooped. I'm proud to say my home of Tirunelveli, in Tamil Nadu, makes the most popular halwa in India. It has the consistency of Turkish Delight and people come from all over to buy it from confectioner Iruttu Kadai Halwa. Making it is so laborious that my mother didn't believe it was worthwhile teaching Suba how to do it. Thankfully, my mum still makes it for me when I go to visit the family.

Of course, as much as we love them, sweets should be eaten in moderation—an excess causes discontent and yearning, while just the right amount promises satisfaction and longevity.

pistachio kulfi

pistachio ice cream

Kulfi is a very popular North Indian ice cream consumed by all. Traditionally it is served on wooden sticks by street hawkers. Eating kulfi takes Suba back to her childhood days. Back in the 1970s in India, she did not have the luxury of owning a fridge, so her after-school treat on hot days would be kulfi. When she heard the kulfiwalla's bell in the street, she knew "heaven on a stick" was just outside.

The secret of a good kulfi is in the slow freezing—it should not have crystallized icicles. This is achieved by reducing the milk to a nice thick consistency, thereby removing the water from the milk. Today, we have evaporated milk, which is the closest to reduced milk. This recipe uses evaporated milk, but if you feel adventurous, you can use full-cream milk and slowly reduce it to a third. The kulfi survives well in the freezer and can be prepared in bulk and kept for a long time.

3 cups (26 fl oz/750 ml) evaporated milk

½ cup (4 fl oz/120 ml) heavy whipping cream (35% fat)

4¼ oz (120 g) granulated sugar

5 tablespoons pistachio kernels, coarsely crushed, plus extra to garnish

½ teaspoon ground cardamom

STRAWBERRY COULIS

3½ oz (100 g) strawberries, diced

1 oz (30 g) superfine sugar

1 star anise

½ cinnamon stick

SERVES 6 AS A DESSERT

Put the milk, cream, and sugar in a heavy-based saucepan over low heat and cook for 20 minutes, scraping down the sides of the pan regularly.

Add 3 tablespoons of the crushed pistachios and the ground cardamom, then remove from the heat. Press a piece of plastic wrap onto the surface of the milk mixture and set aside to cool.

Pour into takeaway containers (either three larger ones or six smaller ones) or six ½ cup (4 fl oz/125 ml) capacity dariole molds. Cover with the lids or tightly with plastic wrap to prevent crystallization. Put in the freezer until frozen.

To make the strawberry coulis, put all of the ingredients in a saucepan with ½ cup (4 fl oz/125 ml) of water and cook over low heat for about 5 minutes. Once the strawberries are soft, discard the star anise and cinnamon stick and strain the mixture through a fine mesh sieve placed over a bowl. Using the back of a spoon, push the solids through to form a smooth coulis.

Remove the kulfi from the freezer about 10 minutes before serving, then turn out onto individual serving plates, serve with the strawberry coulis, and garnish with the extra crushed pistachios.

Tip: Feel free to experiment with flavors. Some popular ones are rose, saffron, fig, and walnut.

kadai mangai curry

quail with mango curry

4 butterflied quails

1 teaspoon ground turmeric

2 teaspoons finely grated ginger

1 tablespoon ghee (see glossary)

1 teaspoon cumin seeds

½ teaspoon red chili powder

2 dried red chilies

2 teaspoons tamarind pulp
(see glossary)

1 teaspoon coriander seeds,
crushed

1 tablespoon grated palm sugar
(jaggery) or soft brown sugar

1½ tablespoons store-bought sweet
mango chutney

2 tablespoons vegetable or
sunflower oil

3–4 fresh green mango slices
(optional)

SERVES 4

Preheat the oven to 350°F (180°C/Gas 4) and put a baking tray in to heat up.

Rub the quail with a little salt and half of the turmeric and ginger. Set aside to rest for 20 minutes.

Heat the ghee in a frying pan over medium heat. Add the cumin seeds and gently cook for 1 minute. Add the chili powder, dried chilies, tamarind pulp, coriander seeds, and remaining turmeric and ginger and cook for 4 minutes. Season with salt and add the palm sugar and mango chutney and cook for 5–7 minutes, gradually adding about ¾ cup (6 fl oz/185 ml) of water until the sauce is thick enough to coat the quail. Keep warm and set aside.

Heat the oil in a large ovenproof frying pan over high heat, add the quails, skin side down, and sear for 2 minutes, then turn over and cook for 1 more minute. Put the pan in the oven and roast for 4–6 minutes or until the quail is cooked but still moist inside—do not overcook.

Gently reheat the sauce if necessary. Cut each quail in half or quarters and drizzle the sauce over. Serve garnished with the mango.

Tip: If you don't have an ovenproof frying pan to cook the quail in, simply preheat a baking dish or baking tray in the oven and transfer the quail from the pan to the dish or tray to roast.

veal pasanda

rolled veal in almond & saffron sauce

This dish was instrumental in Abhi's getting the recognition from the most important food critic of Sydney in 1994. It is tender veal slices, rolled with sultanas, cashews, and pistachios, and then simmered in a rich saffron and almond sauce.

6 veal slices (scalloppini)

3 tablespoons slivered almonds

2 tablespoons cashews

1 tablespoon finely grated ginger

1 tablespoon crushed garlic

2 tablespoons ghee (see glossary)

3 tablespoons vegetable
or sunflower oil

3–4 green cardamom pods

1 teaspoon red chili powder

2 teaspoons ground coriander

10 saffron threads

2 red onions, sliced

5½ oz (150 g) plain thick
yogurt, beaten

½ cup (3½ fl oz / 100 ml) half-and-half
cream (18% fat)

2 teaspoons roughly
chopped cilantro (coriander)

FILLING

1½ tablespoons milk powder

1 tablespoon cilantro (coriander)
leaves, chopped

1 tablespoon crushed cashews

2 teaspoons pistachio nuts, halved,
plus extra, crushed, to garnish

2 teaspoons sultanas (golden raisins),
roughly chopped

¼ teaspoon ground cardamom

Combine all of the filling ingredients in a bowl, then divide into six portions.

Lay the veal slices on a work surface. Place a portion of filling in the center of each, leaving the edges clear. Fold in two opposite sides over the filling, then begin rolling from an open side and roll up the veal tightly like a spring roll, making sure all sides are seared. Refrigerate for 4 hours.

Meanwhile, soak the almonds and cashews in a bowl of hot water for 1 hour. Drain, then put in a spice grinder and grind into a smooth paste. Set aside.

Combine the ginger and garlic.

Heat the ghee and 1 tablespoon of the oil together in a saucepan over medium heat, add the cardamom, chili powder, ground coriander, and saffron, and when fragrant, add the onion and cook until golden brown. Add the ginger–garlic paste and fry for 2 minutes.

Mix the beaten yogurt with the cashew and almond paste, add to the pan and cook over low heat for 20 minutes, adding ⅓–1 cup (2½–8 fl oz/ 80–250 ml) of water sparingly in stages. Once the oil starts to separate, remove the pan from the heat.

Heat the remaining oil in a large frying pan over medium–high heat, add the veal rolls and cook briefly on all sides, adding a little salt to taste (see tip).

Pour the sauce over the veal and cook for 2 minutes. Stir in the cream and serve garnished with the chopped cilantro.

Tip: As veal is a prime cut of meat with little fat, it cooks quickly, so be careful not to overcook it and keep in mind that it will cook further in the sauce.

wagyu beef ullathu

keralan beef fry

This is a modern take on the traditional Keralan beef ullathu, using the great wagyu reared in Australia. There are a few steps in this recipe, but it isn't laborious and the results are remarkable. Once the chickpeas are cooked, it is a quick and simple dish to make. The beef needs to be cooked just before serving and the dish finished at the last minute, so make sure you have everything ready.

½ cup (3¼ oz/95 g) black chickpeas (kala chana) (see glossary), soaked overnight and drained, or 1¼ cups (7¾ oz/220 g) canned chickpeas, rinsed and drained

1 teaspoon ground fennel

2 teaspoons ground black pepper

1 teaspoon ground turmeric

2 teaspoons red chili powder

1 tablespoon ground coriander

⅓ cup (2½ fl oz/80 ml) vegetable or sunflower oil

juice of 1 lime

2 lb 4 oz (1 kg) wagyu beef, cut into 4½ oz (125 g) medallions

1 teaspoon black mustard seeds

1 teaspoon fennel seeds

2 teaspoons coriander seeds, coarsely crushed

6 dried red chilies

1 teaspoon black peppercorns, coarsely crushed

2 red onions, chopped

1 tablespoon finely grated ginger

1 tablespoon sliced garlic

3 tablespoons fresh coconut strips or dried coconut flakes

10 curry leaves

2-inch (5-cm) piece of ginger, finely shredded

You will need to begin this recipe a day ahead.

If using black chickpeas, cook in salted water over medium heat for about 2 hours or until tender. Drain and set aside. This can be done the day before and the chickpeas kept in the fridge. If using canned chickpeas, do not cook.

Meanwhile, combine the ground fennel, ground pepper, turmeric, chili powder, ground coriander, 1½ tablespoons of the oil, and three-quarters of the lime juice in a small nonmetallic bowl, rub the mixture all over the beef, and leave to marinate in the fridge for 1 hour (see tip).

Heat the remaining oil in a frying pan over medium heat, add the mustard and fennel seeds, and let them crackle for about 20 seconds. Add the coriander seeds, dried chilies, and peppercorns and cook for 1 minute. Add the onion and cook for 6–8 minutes or until golden brown. Add the ginger and garlic and cook for 3 minutes.

Chargrill the beef as desired (preferably medium–rare to medium). Remove from the heat and set aside to rest.

Add the chickpeas and coconut strips to the onion mixture, increase the heat to high, add the beef, tossing to coat with the onion mixture, chickpeas, and coconut strips. Toss until everything is combined and heated through, then remove from the heat and add the remaining lime juice and the curry leaves and ginger. Serve immediately.

Tip: Do not add salt to the marinade at this stage, as it will dehydrate the meat.

wattalappam

jaggery baked custard

This dessert originates from the Keralite Muslim populace. It is now a popular Sri Lankan dessert. It is made with kithul jaggery, which is dark brown and slightly bitter in taste, but when paired with the sweetness of the coconut milk, it provides a great balance of taste and color.

½ cup (3¾ oz/110 g) granulated sugar

1 tablespoon cashews, roughly chopped

2 cups (17 fl oz/500 ml) coconut milk

1½ cups (6 oz/175 g) grated kithul jaggery (see glossary)

½ teaspoon ground cardamom

¼ teaspoon ground mace

5 eggs, lightly beaten (see tip)

SERVES 8 AS A DESSERT

Preheat the oven to 315°F (160°C/Gas 2–3).

Put the sugar in a frying pan over medium–high heat and allow to melt, swirling the pan occasionally, but do not stir. Cook until it is a light golden caramel, then quickly but carefully pour the caramel into eight ½ cup (4 fl oz/125 ml) capacity ramekins and swirl around to coat the base of the ramekins. Sprinkle the cashews over the caramel. Set aside.

Put the coconut milk, jaggery, cardamom, and mace in a large mixing bowl and beat well for 4–5 minutes or until the jaggery has dissolved. Stir in the eggs, then strain the mixture through a fine mesh sieve into a jug. Pour the liquid into the prepared ramekins and put in a roasting tray. Pour hot water into the tray to come about halfway up the sides of the ramekins.

Bake for 20 minutes, then reduce the oven temperature to 275°F (140°C/Gas 1) and bake for another 15–20 minutes or until the wattalappam are set.

Remove carefully from the oven and the water bath and cool, then refrigerate.

Bring to room temperature before serving. To remove the wattalappam, gently push down the sides of the custard to release it from the ramekin, then dip the ramekins in hot water and invert onto individual serving plates.

Tip: Do not aerate the eggs by beating them too much, as a good wattalappam should have no air bubbles. It should resemble the texture of a crème caramel.

kanavai nerachathu

stuffed squid with spiced tomato coulis

12 baby squid

2 tablespoons vegetable oil

baby cilantro (coriander) leaves,
to garnish

SPICED TOMATO COULIS

1 tablespoon sunflower oil

½ teaspoon fennel seeds

3 dried red chilies

⅓ cup (3¼ oz/90 g) tomato paste
(concentrated purée)

½ bunch cilantro (coriander),
leaves roughly chopped

juice of 1 lime

STUFFING

1 tablespoon vegetable oil

6 French shallots (eschalots),
finely chopped

1 teaspoon chopped ginger

4 garlic cloves, crushed

3½ oz (100 g) raw shrimp meat,
chopped

1 tomato, finely chopped

2 small green chilies, chopped

½ bunch cilantro (coriander),
leaves roughly chopped

2 tablespoons chickpea
flour (besan)

1 tablespoon tamarind pulp

½ teaspoon ground turmeric

SERVES 6 AS PART OF A SHARED MEAL

First clean the squid. Gently pull the tentacles away from the tube (the intestines should come away at the same time) and set aside. Remove the intestines from the tentacles by cutting under the eyes, then remove the beak, using your fingers to push up the center. Reserve the tentacles. Pull away the quill (the transparent cartilage) from inside the body and remove. Remove and discard the white membrane from the body. Slice off the wings and reserve.

To make the stuffing, heat the oil in a frying pan over medium heat, add the shallot and cook, without browning, for 3 minutes. Add the ginger and garlic and cook for less than a minute. Add the remaining stuffing ingredients, including the squid wings, and cook over medium–high heat for 2 minutes or until you have a dry-ish mixture. Remove from the heat, season with salt, and set aside to cool.

Stuff the squid tubes with the stuffing and skewer the openings with toothpicks to secure. Set aside.

To make the spiced tomato coulis, heat the oil in a small saucepan over medium heat, add the fennel and dried chilies and cook for 1 minute or until fragrant and the tips of the chilies blacken. Add the tomato paste and 1 cup (8 fl oz/250 ml) of water and cook over medium heat for 5–7 minutes. Stir in the cilantro and lime juice and remove from the heat.

Meanwhile, heat the oil in a frying pan over high heat. Add the stuffed squid and tentacles and sear each side. This will only take a couple of minutes, as the filling is already cooked and you only need to cook the outside—do not overcook the squid or they will become rubbery. Serve the squid immediately with a little of the coulis drizzled over the plate and garnished with the cilantro leaves.

sand whiting caldin

goan fish curry

*I ate this dish in a little shack in Goa called Filsumai. The Goan duo of Johnny Gonzalves
and Aunty Lourds run this little joint showcasing their great passion for Goan cuisine.
This is my take on the fish caldin I had there.*

**4 whole sand whiting (or Pacific
whiting), cleaned, gutted,
and scaled**

1½ teaspoons ground turmeric

**3 tablespoons vegetable or
sunflower oil**

2 onions, chopped

**2 small green chilies, halved
lengthwise**

1 tomato, chopped

**1 tablespoon tamarind pulp
(see glossary)**

**⅓ cup (2½ fl oz/80 ml)
coconut milk**

PASTE

**½ cup (1½ oz/45 g) shredded
coconut**

4 garlic cloves, crushed

2 tablespoons coriander seeds

1 tablespoon finely grated ginger

1 tablespoon cumin seeds

1 tablespoon black peppercorns

3 dried red chilies

**1 tablespoon white poppy seeds
(see glossary)**

SERVES 4 AS PART OF A SHARED MEAL

Cut each fish into three pieces. Rub with a little of the ground
turmeric and set aside for 20 minutes.

To make the paste, place all of the ingredients in a small
blender and process until finely ground. Add ½ cup (4 fl oz/
125 ml) of water and blend to a smooth paste. Set aside.

Heat the oil in a heavy-based saucepan over medium heat, add
the onion and cook for 6–8 minutes or until light brown. Add the
chilies, tomato, and prepared paste, stir and cook for 15 minutes or
until the raw coconut smell is gone.

Add the fish, tamarind pulp, and sufficient water to only just
cover the fish, season with salt, and cook for 5–7 minutes.

Add the coconut milk and cook for 5 minutes. Serve
immediately.

Tip: The coconut milk is added towards the end so it retains
its sweetness.

quail porichadu

pan-seared quail

1 tablespoon ground coriander

1 teaspoon ground cumin

½ teaspoon ground turmeric

1 teaspoon red chili powder

1 teaspoon garam masala
(see page 125)

juice of 1 lemon

1 tablespoon finely grated ginger

1 teaspoon crushed garlic

4 butterflied quails

3 tablespoons vegetable oil

1 teaspoon fennel seeds

2 dried red chilies

1 red onion, sliced

1 potato, thinly sliced

20 curry leaves

finely shredded ginger, to serve

SERVES 4 AS PART OF A SHARED MEAL

Preheat the oven to 350°F (180°C/Gas 4).

Combine the coriander, cumin, turmeric, chili powder, garam masala, lemon juice, ginger, and garlic and rub all over the quails. Set aside to marinate for 20 minutes.

Heat 1 tablespoon of the oil in a large ovenproof frying pan (see tip) over medium heat, add the fennel and chilies, and cook until the tips of the chilies blacken. Add the onion and cook for 6–8 minutes or until golden brown.

While the onion is being cooked, heat 1 tablespoon of oil in a frying pan over medium–high heat and quickly fry the sliced potato. Set aside.

Add the quails, skin side down, to the pan with the onion and sear for 2 minutes, then turn over and sear for 1 minute. Towards the end, add half of the curry leaves and the fried potato and toss to combine.

Put the pan in the oven and roast 4–6 minutes or until the quail is cooked but still moist inside—do not overcook.

Meanwhile, heat the remaining oil in a frying pan over low heat, add the curry leaves, and cook until just crisp. Drain on a paper towel and set aside.

Serve the quail garnished with the fried curry leaves and ginger.

Tip: If you don't have an ovenproof frying pan to cook the quail in, simply preheat a baking dish or baking tray in the oven and transfer the quail mixture from the pan to the dish to roast.

lau chingri

shrimp with winter melon

I came across this dish through the Indian Consul General, Amit Dasgupta, a frequent diner at Aki's and a passionate food enthusiast. He enjoys sharing his culinary knowledge and has been kind enough to pass on his mother's recipe. I find this dish to have a lot of clean and simple flavors where the ingredients speak for themselves. It is a quick and easy dish to prepare and is one of my favorites. It's best cooked with small prawns. The traditional recipe asks for the prawns to be cooked whole because of the size. They are cooked to a crunchy texture and provide an excellent counterpoint to the melon.

½ cup (3½ fl oz/100 ml) vegetable or sunflower oil, for shallow-frying

1 lb 5 oz (600 g) shrimp, heads removed and legs trimmed

1 dried bay leaf

3 dried red chilies

½ teaspoon granulated sugar

1½ teaspoons panch phoran masala (see glossary)

1 tablespoon finely grated ginger

7 oz (200 g) winter melon (also called ash gourd), peeled, halved lengthwise, sliced with seeds removed

2 teaspoons ground cumin

juice of 1 lime

SERVES 4–6 AS PART OF A SHARED MEAL

Heat the oil in a large deep-sided frying pan over high heat, add the shrimp in small batches, and shallow-fry until crisp. Remove with a slotted spoon and drain on a paper towel. Set aside.

Discard all but 3 tablespoons of the oil in the pan and heat over medium heat. Add the bay leaf, dried chilies, sugar, and panch phoran masala and cook for 1 minute. Stir in the ginger, add the winter melon and cook, covered, for about 10 minutes or until the winter melon is tender. Stir in the cumin.

Toss in the shrimp, season with salt, and increase the heat to evaporate any excess liquid. Add lime juice to taste and serve.

craб iддiappam

coconut crab with steamed rice noodle cakes

Iddiappam are also known as string hoppers in Sri Lankan cooking. You will need specialty iddiappam flour and an iddiappam mold (or a pasta machine). These are both available from Indian and Sri Lankan grocery stores.

COCONUT BROTH

1 tomato

1 tablespoon vegetable
or sunflower oil

½ teaspoon black mustard seeds

½ teaspoon fennel seeds

½ teaspoon fenugreek seeds

1 red onion, thinly sliced

2 small green chilies,
halved lengthwise

½ teaspoon ground turmeric

6 curry leaves

1 teaspoon finely grated ginger

1⅓ cups (11¼ fl oz/330 ml)
coconut milk

CRAB TOPPING

2 teaspoons vegetable
or sunflower oil

1 teaspoon black mustard seeds

1 teaspoon finely grated ginger

½ teaspoon fennel seeds

2 red onions, finely chopped

1 small green chili, chopped

½ teaspoon ground turmeric

7 oz (200 g) cooked blue
swimmer crab meat

1 handful freshly grated
(or frozen) coconut (see glossary)

10 curry leaves

IDDIAPPAMS

1 cup (7 oz/200 g) iddiappam
flour (see glossary)

1 teaspoon vegetable or sunflower oil,
plus extra for greasing

To make the coconut broth, score a shallow cross in the base of the tomato. Put in a heatproof bowl and cover with boiling water. Leave for 30 seconds, then transfer to cold water and peel the skin away from the cross. Cut the tomato in half, scoop out the seeds with a teaspoon and discard. Roughly dice the flesh and set aside.

Heat the oil in a large heavy-based saucepan over medium heat, add the mustard seeds and let them crackle for 20 seconds. Add the fennel and fenugreek, onion, and green chili and cook for about 5 minutes or until the onion starts to soften. Add the turmeric, curry leaves, and ginger, stir to combine, then add the tomato and coconut milk and cook for 10 minutes.

Add ¾ cup (5¼ fl oz/160 ml) of water, as you want a light broth that is not too thick or coconuty, and cook for 5 minutes, then season with salt. Strain the broth through a sieve and discard the solids. Set aside.

To make the iddiappams, bring 1–1¼ cups (9–10¾ fl oz/250–310 ml) of water to a boil. Add a pinch of salt and the oil. Put the flour in a large bowl and very gradually add the boiled water to make a soft dough. Knead well and form into a ball.

Grease the inside of an iddiappam mold with oil and fill with fist-sized portions of the dough at a time. When you press the mold, the dough will begin to fall out in strings. Move the mold in a circular motion, so that the strings fall onto a steaming tray to form a 3-inch (7.5-cm) diameter circle—it should be a thin layer of strings, only one or two layers thick. If using a pasta maker, keep the noodles as thin as possible, finer than angel hair pasta, more like vermicelli. Repeat with the remaining dough. You should have 12 iddiappams. Steam the iddiappams for 10–15 minutes. Keep warm.

To prepare the crab topping, heat the oil in a heavy-based frying pan over medium–high heat, add the mustard seeds and let them crackle for about 20 seconds. Add the ginger, fennel, onion, green chili, and turmeric. Add the crab meat and just enough of the coconut broth to moisten the crab, and toss to combine. Add the fresh coconut and curry leaves and remove from the heat.

To serve, put two iddiappams on each plate. Top with some crab mixture and spoon over a little of the coconut broth to moisten. Serve accompanied by a small ramekin of additional coconut broth for spooning over during eating.

duck seekh kebabs

grilled minced duck kebabs

Wanting a variation from the usual lamb and beef kebab theme, I created this recipe using duck breast meat for its light gaminess and lower fat content than other parts of the duck. It's a lightly spiced kebab, as I want to highlight the flavor of the meat and not cover it up with spicing. The sweetness of the plum chutney complements the light spicing. Easy to prepare and great to eat.

14 oz (400 g) ground duck breast (ask your butcher to do this)

2 teaspoons finely grated orange zest

2 teaspoons finely chopped mint

1 tablespoon finely chopped cilantro (coriander)

½ teaspoon fennel seeds

2 teaspoons finely grated ginger

2 small red chilies, finely chopped

6 bamboo skewers, soaked in water for 20 minutes (see tip)

vegetable or sunflower oil, for brushing

fresh plum slices, to serve

plum chutney (see page 211), to serve

MAKES 6 SMALL KEBABS

Combine the duck, orange zest, herbs, fennel, ginger, and chili with a little salt in a bowl and mix well. Refrigerate for 1 hour. The mixture will be easier to work with if the meat is chilled.

Divide the mixture into six portions and mold each around a bamboo skewer.

Preheat a barbecue grill to medium. Lightly brush the grill with oil and cook the skewers for about 10 minutes, turning occasionally until golden brown and cooked through. Serve with the fresh plum slices and plum chutney.

Tip: Soaking the skewers for 20 minutes will prevent them from burning during cooking.

Feel free to experiment with how to cook the kebabs. Charcoal-fired barbecues will impart a lovely smoky flavor, which will go well with the duck meat, or you could use a chargrill pan. Whichever method you choose, take care not to overcook the meat, otherwise it will be dry.

scallops tamateri

seared scallops with tomato chutney

The sweetness of the scallops marries the tomato chutney perfectly, and the subtle, mellow hint of the curry leaf–infused olive oil is the finishing touch. The chutney is my grandmother's recipe, except I have added onions, which she did not use in her cooking.

12–16 scallops

½ teaspoon ground turmeric

2 tablespoons vegetable oil

CURRY LEAF–INFUSED OIL

1 tablespoon gingili (unscented sesame oil) (see glossary) or sunflower oil

15 curry leaves

2 tablespoons extra virgin olive oil

TOMATO CHUTNEY

6 ripe roma (plum) tomatoes

2 tablespoons gingili (unscented sesame oil) or sunflower oil

3 dried red chilies

½ teaspoon black mustard seeds

½ teaspoon cumin seeds

1 red onion, diced

2 teaspoons Kashmiri chili powder (see glossary)

⅛ teaspoon asafetida (see glossary)

1 tablespoon finely grated ginger

10 curry leaves

1 teaspoon granulated sugar (optional)

SERVES 3–4 AS PART OF A SHARED MEAL

To make the curry leaf–infused oil, heat the gingili in a frying pan over low heat and cook the curry leaves for 30–40 seconds or until crisp. Drain on a paper towel and pat dry to remove the excess oil. Crush using a mortar and pestle and mix with the olive oil. The oil will keep for up to two weeks.

Rub the scallops with the turmeric and set aside for 20 minutes.

Meanwhile, to make the tomato chutney, score a shallow cross in the base of the tomatoes. Put in a heatproof bowl and cover with boiling water. Leave for 30 seconds, then transfer to cold water and peel the skin away from the cross. Cut the tomatoes in half, scoop out the seeds with a teaspoon and discard. Roughly chop the flesh and set aside.

Heat the gingili in a small saucepan over medium heat, add the chilies, and cook until the tips of the chilies turn black. Add the mustard seeds and let them crackle for about 20 seconds. Add the cumin and onion and cook for 5 minutes without browning. Add the chili powder, asafetida, ginger, curry leaves, tomatoes, and ½ cup (3½ fl oz/100 ml) of water (to soften the tomatoes) and cook for 15–20 minutes. If the tomatoes are not sweet enough, add the sugar.

To cook the scallops, heat the oil in a frying pan over high heat, and sear the scallops for about 20 seconds on one side, then turn over and sear the other side for 20 seconds—do not overcook or they will become rubbery.

Serve the scallops on a bed of the chutney, drizzled with the curry leaf–infused oil.

tesri sukhé

goan clams

What a way to celebrate the fresh cashew fenny (fermented cashew liquor) at the residence of our dear friends Seema and Gautam in Goa. Seema was kind enough to share this typical home recipe with me without any hesitation.

This simple recipe does not involve any grinding of spices, major marination, or much mise-en-place. In Goa, the local fishermen will open the clams with a special sickle, like a knife, for you. Here I have substituted baby clams in place of the Goan clams.

3 tablespoons vegetable or sunflower oil

2 teaspoons crushed garlic

2 red onions, sliced into rings

½ teaspoon ground turmeric

1 teaspoon Kashmiri chili powder (see glossary)

2 lb 4 oz (1 kg) baby clams, soaked in water for 1 hour, then drained

2 pieces kokam (see glossary), soaked in 3 tablespoons water, or 2 teaspoons tamarind pulp

½ cup (2½ oz/70 g) grated coconut (see glossary)

½ bunch cilantro (coriander), leaves roughly chopped

green chilies, to garnish (optional)

SERVES 4–6 AS PART OF A SHARED MEAL

Heat the oil in a frying pan over medium heat. Add the garlic and lightly brown, then immediately add the onion, reserving a small handful to garnish, and cook for about 5 minutes or until soft. Add the turmeric and chili powder and cook for 2 minutes.

Add the clams, a pinch of salt, the kokam and its soaking water, and ½ cup (4 fl oz/125 ml) of water and cook, covered, for 2–3 minutes or until the clams open.

Add the coconut and cook for 2–5 minutes, ensuring you do not brown the coconut. Add the cilantro, reserved onion, and chilies to garnish.

kumro phool bhajja

bengali pumpkin flower fritters

In Bengali cuisine, a bhajja (fritter) is an essential part of any meal. A typical Bengali plate will have some rice in the center, surrounded by some fritters, a lentil dish, and some vegetables. On one of my trips to Kolkata (Calcutta) I came across pumpkin flowers at the Lake Market (the city's fish and vegetable center). They piqued my curiosity, as they were sold alongside the vegetables and looked much like zucchini flowers. I asked my Bengali chef friends how they were used and learned that they transform the pumpkin flower into a bhajja. Here's my take on their recipe.

12 pumpkin flowers or zucchini flowers with baby zucchini attached

vegetable oil, for deep-frying

tamarind and ginger chutney (see page 210), to serve

FILLING

¼ cup (2½ oz/75 g) paneer (curd cheese) (see glossary), crumbled, or cottage cheese

2 teaspoons chopped cilantro (coriander) leaves

2 teaspoons golden raisins (sultanas)

1 teaspoon finely grated ginger

BATTER

¾ cup (3¼ oz/90 g) chickpea flour (besan)

3 tablespoons rice flour

½ teaspoon finely grated ginger

½ teaspoon poppy seeds

½ teaspoon cumin seeds

¼ teaspoon red chili powder

⅛ teaspoon ground turmeric

SERVES 4–6 AS A STARTER OR AS PART
OF A SHARED MEAL

To make the filling, crumble the paneer into a bowl, add the remaining ingredients, season with salt, and combine.

Take 2 teaspoons of the filling and use to fill each pumpkin flower. Ensure you do not overstuff the flowers or they will become soggy when fried. Set aside.

To make the batter, place all of the ingredients in a bowl and stir in ¾ cup (6 fl oz/185 ml) of water. Season with salt and gently mix to form a batter, ensuring it is not too runny.

Fill a deep-fryer or large saucepan one-third full with oil and heat to about 355°F (180°C) or until a cube of bread turns golden brown in 15 seconds. Dip the stuffed flowers, in batches, into the batter, coating them completely, and deep-fry for about 3 minutes or until golden brown, turning once to cook evenly. Remove with a slotted spoon and drain on a paper towel. Serve immediately with the tamarind and ginger chutney.

sura puttu

fish hash curry

*This is a common Southern Indian dish that you'll find in small restaurants all over the region.
It is eaten as an accompaniment to a meal with other vegetables, lentils, and rice.*

2 teaspoons ground turmeric

**1 lb 5 oz (600 g) hake fillets,
skin removed**

**3 tablespoons vegetable
or sunflower oil**

½ teaspoon black mustard seeds

½ teaspoon fennel seeds

3 small green chilies, chopped

**1½ tablespoons finely
chopped ginger**

8 garlic cloves, crushed

15 curry leaves

**½ bunch cilantro (coriander),
leaves roughly chopped**

juice of 1 lime

SERVES 6 AS A SIDE DISH

Half-fill a saucepan with water, add 1 teaspoon of the turmeric, and season with salt. Bring to a boil, add the fish, and cook for 5 minutes. Drain the fish, then flake into pieces. Set aside.

Heat the oil in a heavy-based frying pan over medium–high heat, add the mustard seeds and let them crackle for about 20 seconds. Add the fennel seeds, chili, ginger, garlic, and remaining turmeric and cook for 1 minute, stirring regularly so the spices don't burn.

Add the fish and toss together. Add the curry leaves, cilantro, and lime juice. Check the seasoning and serve hot.

maan porrial

venison porrial

⅓ cup (2½ fl oz/80 ml) vegetable
or sunflower oil

1 lb 12 oz (800 g) venison
loin, diced

1 teaspoon black mustard seeds

1 teaspoon fennel seeds

2 red onions, chopped

1 tablespoon finely grated ginger

1 tablespoon sliced garlic

1 teaspoon ground fennel

2 teaspoons cracked black pepper

1 teaspoon ground turmeric

2 teaspoons red chili powder

1 tablespoon ground coriander

1 potato, boiled and diced

½ cup (1½ oz/45 g) shredded
coconut

juice of 1 lime

10 curry leaves

SERVES 4–6 AS PART OF A SHARED MEAL

Heat the oil in a heavy-based frying pan over high heat, add the venison in small batches, and sear the meat all over to prevent the release of the juices during cooking. This is a dry dish and we do not want the venison to sauce it up. Remove from the pan and set aside.

Add the mustard and fennel to the same pan over medium heat and let the mustard seeds crackle for about 20 seconds. Add the onion and cook for 6–8 minutes or until golden brown. Add the ginger and garlic and cook for about 3 minutes.

Add the venison and coat in the mixture. Add the ground fennel, pepper, turmeric, chili powder, ground coriander, potato, and coconut, gently stir to combine, and cook for 5 minutes or until the venison is cooked.

Stir in the lime juice, scatter over the curry leaves, and serve.

punjabi bheh masala

lotus root curry

A very dear family friend from Delhi served us this wonderful dish and shared this recipe with us. That was my first time eating lotus root, and I was extremely fascinated with the texture of the vegetable. This is a North Indian dish, very popular in Kashmir and Punjab. The Kashmiris cook this in yogurt and ghee, while I have made this preparation in mustard oil and poppy seeds.

1 lb 2 oz (500 g) lotus root

2 tablespoons poppy seeds

1 teaspoon ground turmeric

3 tablespoons mustard oil (see glossary)

2 teaspoons cumin seeds

3 red onions, grated

1 tablespoon finely grated ginger

1 teaspoon red chili powder

1 tablespoon ground coriander

3 small green chilies, roughly chopped

red chili powder and finely chopped cilantro (coriander), to garnish (optional)

SERVES 4 AS PART OF A SHARED MEAL

Cut the lotus root into thin slices on an angle and soak in cold water for 1 hour.

Soak the poppy seeds in 3 tablespoons of water for 20 minutes (see tip). Put the poppy seeds and soaking water in a spice grinder or small blender and grind to a fine paste.

Drain the lotus root. Bring a saucepan of water to a boil with ½ teaspoon of the turmeric, add the lotus root, and cook for 20–30 minutes or until soft. Drain and set aside.

Heat 1 tablespoon of the mustard oil in a heavy-based frying pan over medium–high heat, add the cumin and let them crackle for about 20 seconds. Add the onion and cook until brown. Add the poppy seed paste and cook, stirring constantly, for about 3 minutes, adding a little extra oil to prevent the poppy seed paste from sticking to the pan.

Once the onion and poppy seeds turn a darker brown, stir in 1 tablespoon of water. Add the ginger, remaining turmeric, chili powder, and ground coriander and cook over low heat for 5 minutes, stirring regularly.

Add the lotus root and green chili. Keep stirring until the sauce has thickened and coats the lotus root. Season with salt. Garnish with red chili powder and cilantro if desired, and serve.

Tip: Soaking the poppy seeds makes it easier to grind them.

mishti dohi

baked sweet yogurt cream

I discovered this dish on my recent travels to Kolkata (Calcutta). Traditionally, these are baked in clay pots, which aids setting, but then the pot is broken when you've finished (for hygiene, so it's not reused). We were served this for breakfast and I was enamored. What an excellent way to start the day or finish a meal.

½ cup (3½ fl oz/100 ml) thick (double/heavy) cream (crème fraîche can be substituted)

½ cup (4½ oz/130 g) sweetened condensed milk

6½ tablespoons (3½ oz/100 g) plain, thick yogurt

½ teaspoon ground cardamom

1 tablespoon coarsely ground pistachio nuts (optional)

3 tablespoons pomegranate seeds (optional)

SERVES 4 FOR BREAKFAST OR AS A DESSERT

Preheat the oven to 350°F (180°C/Gas 4).

Put the cream, milk, yogurt, and cardamom in a bowl and mix thoroughly, then strain through a sieve into another bowl.

Divide the mixture among four ⅓ cup (2½ fl oz/80 ml) capacity ramekins and put in a baking dish. Pour hot water into the dish to come about halfway up the sides of the ramekins.

Bake for 15–20 minutes or until firmly set, keeping an eye on them. Remove from the water bath and leave to cool to room temperature.

Serve in the ramekins at room temperature or chilled, garnished with the pistachio nuts and pomegranate seeds.

ledikeni

bengali semolina doughnuts

On our recent visit to Kolkata (Calcutta), we came across this dessert that resembles gulab jamun (fried doughnuts soaked in syrup) but is slightly different. Ledikeni is the traditional Bengali dessert called pantua, but it was renamed in honor of Lady Canning, wife of Governor-General Charles Canning, who visited the local sweet shops of Calcutta in 1856.

2⅔ cups (1 lb 2 oz /500 g) granulated sugar

3 teaspoons rosewater

12 oz (350 g) paneer (curd cheese) (see glossary) (see tip)

2 tablespoons fine semolina

1⅓ cups (5½ oz/150 g) milk powder

3 tablespoons self-rising flour

3 black cardamom pods, seeds only (see tip)

2¼ cups (1 lb 2 oz/500 g) ghee, melted (see glossary)

3½ oz (100 g) superfine sugar

18 raisins

SERVES 6 AS A DESSERT

Put the granulated sugar, rosewater, and 1 cup (8 fl oz/250 ml) of water in a saucepan over medium heat and slowly bring to a boil, stirring to dissolve the sugar. Continue to boil for 3 minutes. Set aside to cool slightly (see tip).

Put the paneer, semolina, milk powder, flour, cardamom seeds, 1 tablespoon of the ghee, and 2 tablespoons of the superfine sugar in a large bowl and knead to a doughy consistency. Set aside for 15 minutes.

Portion the dough into 18 balls. Push a raisin into the center of each ball and roll into a cylindrical shape.

Heat the remaining ghee in a wok or heavy-based saucepan to 320°F (160°C) or until a cube of bread browns in 30–35 seconds. Fry the dough balls for about 3 minutes, turning occasionally until slightly darker than golden brown. Remove with a slotted spoon and drain on a paper towel. Immerse the cooked dough in the prepared sugar syrup and leave to soak for 2 hours.

To serve, sprinkle the remaining superfine sugar onto a large sheet of baking paper. Remove the balls from the syrup, allowing the excess to drip off, and roll in the sugar.

Tip: You can substitute the paneer with fresh ricotta cheese.

Green cardamoms can be substituted for the black version.

The temperature of the sugar syrup should be slightly on the warmer side, so when the doughnuts are added to it, the syrup will be able to seep through and flavor them.

pineapple kesari

pineapple semolina cake

This is a dessert that is very close to my heart. It has been a favorite of mine since childhood, but it became more special when my prospective mother-in-law served it to me when I met Suba for the first time. It is a popular sweet in South India and is one of those dishes that can be quickly conjured up if an unannounced visitor lands on your doorstep.

½ cup (4½ oz/125 g) ghee, melted (see glossary)

½ oz (15 g) cashew nuts, chopped into small pieces

¾ cup (5½ oz/150 g) coarse semolina (see tip)

1½ cups (10½ oz/300 g) superfine sugar

10 saffron threads

1¾ oz (50 g) pineapple, finely diced

3 green cardamom pods, crushed

2 tablespoons golden raisins (sultanas)

SERVES 6–8 AS A DESSERT

Place 1 tablespoon of the ghee in a small frying pan over medium heat and fry the cashews until golden brown. Set aside.

Heat a large, dry, heavy-based saucepan over low heat, add the semolina, and lightly toast for 1 minute to remove the moisture. Add 1¾ cups (14 fl oz/400 ml) of water and cook for about 5–7 minutes, stirring constantly. Once the semolina has softened, add the sugar, saffron, pineapple, and cardamom pods—this will turn the mixture a little watery. Gently cook for 4–5 minutes or until the sugar has dissolved, stirring constantly so the sugar does not caramelize on the bottom.

Slowly pour the remaining ghee into the semolina and cook for 5 minutes. By this point, the mixture should leave the sides of the pan and not stick to the base. It should appear a bit oily (see tip).

Stir half of the fried cashews and all of the raisins into the semolina and serve warm with the remaining cashews sprinkled over the top. This is a very sweet dish, so you only need a small portion per person.

Tip: Coarse semolina is preferred over the fine variety.

The kesari should not be sticky to the fingers. There is a generous amount of ghee used so it does not stick to the eating utensils and for its great taste.

You can replace the pineapple with other flavors such as apricot and candied ginger.

condiments
& sides

green chutney

coriander & chili chutney

½ bunch mint, leaves picked

1 bunch cilantro (coriander), leaves picked and coarsely chopped

4 long green chilies, chopped

½ red onion

1 tablespoon lemon juice

2 teaspoons finely grated ginger

MAKES ABOUT 1½ CUPS

Process all of the ingredients with 1 teaspoon of salt and ½ teaspoon of ground black pepper in a food processor until smooth. Transfer to a small bowl and cover until ready to serve.

tamarind & ginger chutney

3 tablespoons gingili (unscented sesame oil) (see glossary)

6 dried red chilies

1 teaspoon black mustard seeds

2 tablespoons finely grated ginger

⅓ cup (2½ fl oz/80 ml) tamarind concentrate (see glossary)

1 cup (5½ oz/150 g) grated palm sugar (jaggery)

MAKES ABOUT 1½ CUPS

Heat the gingili in a small saucepan over medium–high heat, add the chilies and cook until blackened. Add the mustard seeds and allow them to crackle for 20 seconds.

Add the ginger, tamarind concentrate, and scant 1 cup (7 fl oz/ 200 ml) of water and bring to a boil. Add the palm sugar and cook for 20 minutes or until it is thick enough to coat a spoon. Remove from the heat and set aside to cool. Store in an airtight jar in the fridge for up to two weeks.

plum chutney

1 lb 2 oz (500 g) red plums, finely
diced with stones removed

7 tablespoons (3½ fl oz/100 ml)
white vinegar

½ cup (3½ oz/100 g) granulated
sugar

1 cinnamon stick

2–3 green cardamom pods

2–3 black peppercorns

2 teaspoons (⅛ oz/3–4 g)
Kashmiri chili powder
(see glossary)

pinch of finely chopped garlic

MAKES ABOUT 2½ CUPS

Combine all of the ingredients in a saucepan over low heat and
cook for 15–20 minutes or until thickened, stirring occassionally.
Remove from the heat, then transfer to the fridge to chill. Serve
cold. Store in an airtight container in the fridge for up to a week.

burrani raita

2 cups (1 lb 2½ oz/520 g) plain,
thick yogurt

12 garlic cloves

½ teaspoon red chili powder

3 tablespoons milk

ground cumin, to garnish

MAKES ABOUT 2 CUPS

Beat the yogurt until smooth. Set aside.

Crush the garlic, then pass through a fine sieve to collect the
juice. Discard the solids.

Add the garlic juice and chili powder to the yogurt, season with
salt, and mix well. Add enough milk to achieve a thin consistency.
Chill until ready to serve.

Garnish with a pinch of cumin and serve with biriyani.

chettiyar chutney

6 onions, roughly chopped

10 roma (plum) tomatoes, peeled and roughly chopped

8–10 dried red chilies

2⅓ cup (9¾ oz/275 g) tamarind concentrate (see glossary)

⅓ cup (2½ oz/75 g) chana dal, toasted (see glossary)

8 thin garlic slices

1 tablespoon gingili (unscented sesame oil) (see glossary)

1 teaspoon black mustard seeds

MAKES ABOUT 1½ CUPS

Place all of the ingredients except the gingili and mustard seeds in a food processor and process until finely chopped and smooth. Transfer to a bowl.

Heat the oil in a frying pan over medium–high heat, add the mustard seeds and allow them to crackle for 20 seconds. Remove from the heat and add to the onion mixture.

mint & yogurt sauce

1 bunch mint, leaves and stalks

1 bunch cilantro (coriander), leaves and stalks

2 small green chilies

2 garlic cloves

1 tablespoon finely grated ginger

1 teaspoon cumin seeds

1 teaspoon granulated sugar

10 black peppercorns

2 cups (1 lb 2 oz/500 g) plain, thick yogurt

juice of 1 lime

MAKES ABOUT 1½ CUPS

Roughly chop the herb leaves and stalks and place in a food processor. Add the remaining ingredients, except the lime juice and yogurt, and process to a smooth paste, adding minimal water as necessary.

Place the yogurt in a bowl and beat until smooth. Add the herb mixture and lime juice, and season with salt. Refrigerate until needed.

(pictured page 216)

tamarind rice

2½ cups (1 lb 2 oz/500 g) long-grain white rice, rinsed

¾ cup (5¾ fl oz/180 ml) vegetable or sunflower oil

1 teaspoon black mustard seeds

5 dried red chilies

½ teaspoon fenugreek seeds

pinch of asafetida (see glossary)

1 teaspoon ground turmeric

½ cup (4 fl oz/125 ml) tamarind water (see glossary)

1 tablespoon chana dal (see glossary)

1 tablespoon raw peanuts

1 tablespoon coriander seeds, toasted and ground

1 tablespoon sesame seeds, toasted and ground

10 fried curry leaves

SERVES 4

Place the rice in a saucepan, cover with 1 inch (2.5 cm) of water and bring to a boil over medium heat. Once it is three-quarters cooked, drain the rice, spread it over a tray, and allow it to dry completely and cool to room temperature.

Drizzle ⅓ cup (2½ fl oz/80 ml) of the oil over the rice.

Heat ⅓ cup (2½ fl oz/80 ml) of the oil in a small saucepan over medium–high heat, add the mustard seeds and let them crackle for 20 seconds, then add the chilies, fenugreek, asafetida, and turmeric. Add the tamarind water, season with salt, and cook for 3 minutes or until thick like a gravy.

Heat the remaining oil in a small frying pan over medium heat, add the chana dal and peanuts, and cook until golden brown. Add to the rice.

Add the ground coriander seeds and sesame seeds, tamarind mixture, and curry leaves to the rice, mix well, and serve.

lemon rice

2½ cups (1 lb 2 oz/500 g) long-grain white rice, rinsed

1 tablespoon vegetable or sunflower oil

1 teaspoon black mustard seeds

pinch of asafetida (see glossary)

1 teaspoon chana dal (see glossary)

1 teaspoon urad dal (black lentils/black gram) (see glossary)

2 dried red chilies, broken in half

2 small green chilies, chopped

½ teaspoon ground turmeric

juice of 3 lemons

1 tablespoon fried cashew nuts

1 tablespoon fried peanuts

10 fried curry leaves

SERVES 4

Place the rice in a saucepan, cover with 1 inch (2.5 cm) of water, and bring to a boil over medium heat. Cook until al dente. Drain the water and place the rice in a large bowl.

Heat the oil in a small frying pan over medium–high heat, add the mustard seeds and allow them to crackle for 20 seconds, then add the asafetida, chana dal, urad dal, and dried and green chilies, and cook until the dal is golden brown. Add the turmeric, then remove from the heat and set aside to cool to room temperature.

Add the lemon juice to the spice mixture, then pour the mixture over the rice, season with salt, and mix well. Garnish with the fried nuts and curry leaves.

Tip Make sure the mixture has cooled to room temperature before adding the lemon juice, otherwise it will taste bitter.

curd rice

2½ cups (1 lb 2 oz/500 g) long-grain white rice, rinsed

1 tablespoon vegetable oil

½ teaspoon black mustard seeds

1 dried red chili, broken in half

½ cup (4 fl oz/125 ml) milk

3 small green chilies, chopped

1¼-inch (3-cm) piece of ginger, chopped

10 curry leaves

5 cups (3 lb/1.3 kg) fresh curd or plain thick yogurt

SERVES 4

Place the rice in a saucepan, cover with 1 inch (2.5 cm) of water, and bring to a boil over medium heat. Cook until al dente. Drain the water, place the rice in a large bowl, and allow to cool.

Heat the oil in a frying pan over medium–high heat, add the mustard seeds and allow them to crackle for 20 seconds, then add the dried and green chilies, ginger, and curry leaves, and cook until fragrant but not colored. Remove from the heat and add to the rice.

Add the curd, season with salt, and stir, then add the milk and mix thoroughly. This is best eaten with lime pickle.

coconut rice

2½ cups (1 lb 2 oz/500 g) long-grain white rice, rinsed

2 tablespoons coconut oil

½ teaspoon black mustard seeds

pinch of asafetida (see glossary)

1 tablespoon chana dal (see glossary)

1 teaspoon urad dal (black lentils/black gram) (see glossary)

2 dried red chilies, broken in half

1 small green chili, halved lengthwise

1 coconut, flesh grated

10 curry leaves

1 tablespoon fried cashew nuts

SERVES 4

Place the rice in a saucepan, cover with 1 inch (2.5 cm) of water, and bring to a boil over medium heat. Cook until al dente. Drain the water and place the rice in a large bowl.

Heat the oil in a frying pan over medium–high heat, add the mustard seeds and allow them to crackle for 20 seconds, then add the asafetida, chana dal, urad dal, and dried and green chilies, and cook until the dal turns golden brown.

Add the coconut and cook until fragrant but not colored. Remove from the heat, stir in the curry leaves, and season with salt.

Pour the spice mixture over the rice and mix well. Garnish with the fried cashew nuts.

rasam powder

8 dried red chilies

2 tablespoons coriander seeds

20 black peppercorns

1 tablespoon cumin seeds

2 tablespoons toor dal (yellow lentils) (see glossary)

1 tablespoon chana dal (see glossary)

1 teaspoon ground turmeric

MAKES ABOUT ½ CUP

In a dry-frying pan over medium heat, lightly toast all the ingredients, shaking the pan occasionally so they don't burn. Using a spice grinder or mortar and pestle, grind into a fine powder. Store in an airtight jar for up to six months.

chapatis

3⅓ cups (1 lb 2 oz/500 g) all-purpose
flour or wholemeal atta flour
(see glossary)

1 teaspoon salt

1 tablespoon ghee (see glossary)
or butter, for greasing

MAKES 18–20

Sift the flour into a large bowl and make a well in the center. While mixing with your hand, gradually add 1⅓ cup (10½ fl oz/ 300 ml) of water, kneading until a smooth dough forms. Add the salt and knead to combine. Cover with a lid or plastic wrap and set aside for 20–30 minutes.

Lightly knead the dough again, then divide it into 18–20 rounded portions.

With your palms lightly greased with a little ghee, flatten each portion and lightly dust with flour so it doesn't stick to the work surface, then roll it into a thin 5 inch (13 cm) diameter circle using a rolling pin.

Heat a dry-frying pan or tava over medium–high heat. When it is hot, place the chapati in the pan and cook until small air pockets start to bubble up, then turn over and lightly cook the other side.

Once it is cooked on both sides, gently press the sides down using a clean cloth. This will make the chapati swell. Once puffed, remove from the heat and serve hot.

Repeat with the remaining dough.

Tip: You can make the chapatis about 20 minutes ahead of time. Keep them wrapped in a tea towel and store in an airtight container—this will ensure they remain soft. You can also smear some ghee over the top before serving.

(pictured page 216)

puri

1½ cups (8 oz/225 g) all-purpose flour or wholemeal atta flour (see glossary)

1 teaspoon salt

ghee, for greasing (see glossary)

vegetable or sunflower oil, for deep-frying

Sift the flour into a large bowl and make a well in the center. While mixing with your hand, gradually add ½ cup (3½ fl oz/ 100 ml) of water, kneading until a thick dough forms. Add the salt and knead to combine. Cover with a lid or plastic wrap and set aside for 30 minutes.

Lightly knead the dough again, then divide it into portions the size of a golf ball.

With your palms lightly greased with a little ghee, flatten each portion and lightly dust with flour so it doesn't stick to the work surface, then roll it into a thin 3–4 inch (7.5–10 cm) diameter round using a rolling pin. Repeat with the remaining dough balls.

Heat the oil in a small, deep-sided saucepan to 355°F (180°C) or until a cube of bread turns golden brown in 15 seconds, and deep-fry the puri, one at a time. Using a large slotted spoon, keep the puri under the oil. This helps the puri to puff up. Once it is puffed and golden brown, remove from the oil with the slotted spoon and serve immediately. Repeat with the remaining puri.

(pictured page 217)

glossary

amchur *(dry mango powder)* A souring agent widely used in North India. It is derived from powdered sun-dried green mangoes. Used primarily to sprinkle on chaat and tandoori preparations.

asafetida *(hing)* A highly aromatic spice derived from the root of the ferula asafetida plant. It is primarily imported from Iran. Although very pungent in its raw form, adding it to hot oil gives a rich onion-like flavor to dishes. In Hindu cooking, garlic and asafetida are not used together as they provide similar flavors. Asafetida is also used for its medicinal properties as it aids digestion. It is generally used in its powdered form and is available from Indian grocery stores in little containers.

atta flour A high-gluten flour used to make unleavened Indian breads such as chapati, puri, naan, and paratha. It's available at Indian grocery stores.

black chickpeas *(kala chana)* Also known as bengal gram, these are a variety of lentil. Unlike regular chickpeas, these are dark brown in color, smaller in size, and harder. They need to be soaked overnight before cooking. Chana dal is made from black chickpeas by removing the skins and splitting them in half.

black cumin seeds *(jeera)* Cumin comes from the same family as fennel, caraway, and aniseed. It is used whole and in powdered form. It's a delicate spice and will turn bitter if cooked for more than a minute. It is used to temper dry vegetarian dishes and pullaos.

cardamom, *black & green* Green cardamom is sourced mainly from South India and Sri Lanka. It is used whole and in powdered form. It is also one of the main ingredients in a garam masala. Crushed cardamom seeds are also used in sweet dishes. Black cardamom is grown in the Himalayan foothills. It is bigger than its green counterpart and has an earthy/woody flavor. It is used in garam masalas, too, and also in pullaos in North Indian cooking.

carom seeds *(ajwain)* Carom seeds come from the same family of plants as coriander, cumin, and fennel. It is also known as bishop's weed, caraway seeds, or thymol seeds. It is usually used in its seed form, as a flavoring agent in batters and as a part of tempering (tadka). It has a strong flavor and is therefore used in small quantities. Ayurvedics claim it aids digestion and helps to control nausea.

cassia bark Also referred to as Chinese cinnamon, it is an aromatic bark closely related to cinnamon. It is harder than cinnamon and has a darker woody look. It's used in either powdered form or whole, and forms part of garam masalas.

chana dal This is a derivative of the black chickpea where the skin has been removed and the kernel has been split in half. It looks like yellow split peas but is different as it does not readily boil down and collapse like the yellow split peas. It is available at Indian grocery stores.

charoli *(chironji)* Known as chironji in Hindi, it is the soft seed center of a bush cultivated in northwest India. It is primarily used in sweets and as a thickening agent for gravies. It has a sweet flavor.

chili powder, *kashmiri, red & yellow*
Chili is an integral part of all Indian cuisines. There are a variety of chilies and chili powders based on regions, and their use is dictated by their characteristics. The Kashmiri chili is a dark-colored and mild-flavored chili. It imparts a deep red color when used in dishes and is medium hot. It is similar to paprika, but it has more heat. The red chili is the most commonly used chili powder. It provides a strong, biting heat. Add it in small quantities. You can always add a little more later. The yellow chili is primarily used in Northern/Mughlai cuisine. It is used for its yellow color to give a rich golden look to dishes and strong heat.

coconut Coconut is a widely used ingredient in Southern Indian cooking. It is used in a multitude of forms such as: shredded, oil, milk, cream, and paste. It has a sweet flavor and is a good binding agent for some dishes. Freshly grated coconut is the white pulp of a coconut. It is available at Indian grocery stores frozen in packets. Most other forms are readily available in supermarkets.

curry leaves Curry leaves are an important aromatic ingredient in Southern Indian dishes. They can be used fresh or dried, though the fresh leaves are more flavorful. They do not keep well under refrigeration and have a short shelf life. They are usually added to hot oil to release their flavor. They are used for garnishes and tempering.

dried fenugreek leaves *(kasuri methi)* Known as kasuri methi in Hindi, these are the dried leaves of the fenugreek plant. They have a bitter taste and are used in small quantities. They are readily available at Indian grocery stores.

dried kashmiri red chilies *see chili powder, kashimiri, red & yellow*

drumstick The muringa kai (in Tamil) is the long, slender green seed pod of the drumstick tree. It is used widely in Southern Indian dishes. It is very fibrous and has a hard outer skin. It needs to be chopped into segments about 2–3¼ inches (5–8 cm) because the inside of the pod is what we need to cook. The outer shell is not eaten, but is chewed to get to the soft seed and flesh inside. It must be well cooked in sauces. It is readily available at Indian grocery stores fresh, cut, frozen, and canned.

garam masala The word *garam*, meaning "heat," relates to the intensity of spice, and *masala* means a combination of different spices. So garam masala refers to a blend of spices, and can be either whole or powdered. All Indian households would use a garam masala, but the ingredients differ according to recipe requirements and personal choice. A typical Indian garam masala contains black peppercorns, cloves, cinnamon, cumin, and cardamom.

ghee This is clarified butter, readily available in Indian stores. Ghee features prominently in Punjabi cuisine, where it is used to give richness to food. Most Indian sweets are made with ghee. It has a long shelf life and does not need refrigeration.

gingili *(unscented sesame oil)* This is a vegetable oil derived from sesame seeds. Unlike sesame seed oil used in southeastern cuisines, this one has no scent. It is called *nalla ennai* (in Tamil), meaning "good oil."

iddiappam flour Iddiappam is a traditional culinary specialty of South India consisting of rice flour pressed into noodle form, shaped into round cakes, and then steamed. Hand-pounded rice flour is used to make iddiappam. Both white and brown rice flour are used. These are available in South Indian or Sri Lankan grocery stores.

kewra water *(pandanus water)* This is an extract distilled from pandanus flowers. It is a clear liquid, similar to rosewater, and can be used in meat dishes, rice biriyanis, and sweets. It is a strong flavoring, so care must be taken when adding it to preparations. It stores well for up to a year at room temperature and longer if refrigerated. Care must be taken that the cap is sealed well, as the strong scent can be hard to eradicate from other things.

kithul jaggery This is the natural palm sugar of Sri Lanka. It's a dark brown jaggery. It is used as a natural alternative to processed sugar as it is all natural, and free of preservatives and chemicals. It is made from the sap of the young kithul palm. Available in Sri Lankan grocery stores.

kokam A member of the mangosteen family, the kokam bears a purple colored fruit that is used as a souring agent in western coastal cooking. The outer cover of the fruit is sun-dried, and that is used in cooking. It gives a sour taste and a darkish purple color to the dish. The flavor profile is similar to tamarind, which is used more in South India.

moong dal *(green gram)* These are whole green mung beans. These need to be soaked in water before they can be cooked into a dal. This bean is also skinned and split in half to reveal a pale yellow color, and it is used for making pancake batter and yellow-hued dals.

mustard oil This is a fatty vegetable oil used predominantly in Northern Indian cooking. It has a strong, pungent odor and is therefore heated almost to smoking point before cooking in order to reduce the smell and taste. It can be produced from both black mustard and white mustard seeds. Ayurvedics consider it to assist hair regeneration, and improve skin texture and vision.

nigella seeds *(onion seeds/kalonji)* These are small black seeds used in Indian cooking as a mild substitute for pepper. These seeds have very little smell but release their flavor when heated. Nigella seeds are also one of the five ingredients in panch phoran masala (see below). These are not related to onions at all, but the name seems to have stuck from a perception of its onion-like smell.

palm vinegar This is a white, cloudy vinegar made from the fermented sap of the palm flower. It can be used as a substitute for toddy vinegar.

panch phoran masala Literally translated to "five spices," it is a mix of whole spices used in Eastern Indian cooking. The five spices are: fennel, mustard, nigella, fenugreek, and cumin seeds in equal proportions. Fenugreek seeds may be reduced to avoid a bitter taste. Panch phoran masala is usually used whole, not powdered.

paneer This is a fresh cottage cheese made from curdling heated milk by adding lemon juice or vinegar. The curdled milk is then hung in muslin (cheesecloth) and the excess water content (the whey) is drained out of the cheese. The curds can then be pressed into blocks or left in their scrambled form. It's available in the refrigerated section of Indian grocery stores.

paratha This is a generic term for an Indian flatbread made from wholemeal atta or plain flour. There are many types of parathas with different textures or fillings.

roti A staple unleavened Indian bread made from wholemeal atta, usually cooked on a hotplate or griddle.

tamarind, *pulp, concentrate & water*
Tamarind is the pod-like fruit of the tamarind tree. The pulp of the ripened brown pod is extracted for cooking. It is used extensively across India to add a sour and piquant taste to dishes. The pulp is available in Indian stores as a block. This needs to be loosened in hot water to make a thick mixture that is then strained and the resulting "tamarind water" is used in cooking. Indian grocery stores also sell tamarind concentrate, which is basically a ready-made, more concentrated version of the pulp prepared as above.

tempering This is the process by which spices are added to heated oil in order to release their individual flavors. It can be done either at the beginning of a dish or added onto a cooked preparation at the end.

toddy vinegar The toddy vinegar of Goa dates back to the influx of the Portuguese settlers, who introduced fermented palm wine, called toddy. The Christians in Goa use this toddy to make vinegar, which is used in meat and fish dishes as a souring agent. It should be added in the final stages of cooking, as it will turn bitter if cooked for long. It is not readily available outside of Goa, so it may be substituted with either palm or malt vinegar.

toor dal *(yellow lentils)* These are yellow split peas and are used in the preparation of the popular South Indian dish sambar. These are high-protein pulses, which are used heavily across India, predominantly in a vegetarian diet. These cook easily and do not require extended soaking.

urad dal *(black lentils, black gram)* Whole urad dal is a black-skinned pulse that is used to make the popular dal makhni. The whole urad needs to be soaked overnight and then slow-cooked extensively to achieve a rich creamy flavor. In South India, the urad dal is dehulled and split to be used in batters for dosas and idlis. It is also used in the tempering of dishes, as it gives a nutty and crunchy texture.

white poppy seeds Also known as khus-khus, these are used primarily as a thickening agent in Mughlai dishes. The seeds are soaked in water and then ground to a smooth paste.

acknowledgments

A big thanks, "*nanri*" as we say in Tamil, to Murdoch Books, which has helped us in our journey of creating our first cookbook. Our heartiest thanks to Sally Webb and the Murdoch Books team, who took this book as their own, from the beginning to the end. Our thanks to Laura Wilson (Project Editor), Tania Gomes (Designer), Michelle Noerianto (Stylist), Mark Roper (Photographer), Livia Caiazzo (Managing Editor), Belinda So (Editor), Katy Holder (Food Editor), Brett Sargent, Olivia Andrews, and Grace Campbell. Without you guys, the outcome would not have been as beautiful as it is.

To Les Luxford for his support and advice through the years, and also for being kind enough to write the foreword for this book.

To Simon Thompson for editing our story and giving it the voice for our feelings.

To Mohanchandran (Taj General Manager) and Seema, you shall always be remembered for the help you extended to us on our travels to India toward discovering the depth of Indian cuisine.

Thank you to Chef Praveen Anand (Park Sheraton, Chennai), who we could always refer to as our encyclopedia on Southern Indian cuisine for research. We would like to thank all the chefs from India who assisted us in the recipe research: Chef Amit Choudhury (Taj Palace, Delhi), Chef Sujaon Mukherjee (Taj Bengal), Chef Ganesh Joshi (Taj Srinagar), Chef Narendra Singh (Taj Lucknow), and Chef Valentine (Taj Lucknow).

Thanks to Luke Nguyen and Susanna for getting us started on this wonderful project.

Thanks to the teams at Abhi's and Aki's—Chefs Ranjan and Vikram, for their ever-present support. Special thanks to Akshay for all the tireless, late night "recipe cooking" with the right spirit.

index

Thunder Bay Press
An imprint of Printers Row Publishing Group
10350 Barnes Canyon Road, Suite 100, San Diego, CA 92121
www.thunderbaybooks.com

First published in 2013 by Murdoch Books, an imprint of Allen & Unwin
This edition published in 2015 by Thunder Bay Press

Thunder Bay Press is an imprint of Printers Row Publishing Group, a division of Readerlink Distribution Services, LLC. The Thunder Bay Press name and logo are trademarks of Readerlink Distribution Services, LLC.

All notations of errors or omissions should be addressed to Thunder Bay Press, Editorial Department, at the above address. All other correspondence (author inquiries, permissions) concerning the content of this book should be addressed to:

Murdoch Books Australia
83 Alexander Street
Crows Nest, NSW 2065
Australia
murdochbooks.com.au
info@murdochbooks.com.au

Murdoch Books UK
Erico House, 6th Floor
93–99 Upper Richmond Road
Putney, London SW15 2TG
murdochbooks.co.uk
info@murdochbooks.co.uk

For Thunder Bay:
Publisher: Peter Norton
Publishing Team: Lori Asbury, Ana Parker, Laura Vignale
Editorial Team: JoAnn Padgett, Melinda Allman, Traci Douglas
Production Team: Blake Mitchum, Rusty von Dyl

Library of Congress Cataloging-in-Publication Data
Mahadevan, Kumar.
 From India : food, family & tradition / Kumar & Suba Mahadevan. -- 1 [edition].
    pages cm
 Originally published: Crows Nest, NSW : Murdoch Books, 2013.
 Includes bibliographical references and index.
 ISBN 978-1-62686-523-5 (hardcover cloth : alk. paper)
 1. Cooking, Indic. I. Mahadevan, Suba. II. Title.
  TX724.5.I4M32 2015
  641.5954--dc23
                    2015004742

Printed in China.
19 18 17 16 15 1 2 3 4 5

The Publisher and stylist would like to thank Ruby Star Traders for lending their unique Indian homewares and textiles for photography.

IMPORTANT: Those who might be at risk from the effects of salmonella poisoning (the elderly, pregnant women, young children, and those suffering from immune deficiency diseases) should consult their doctor with any concerns about raw eggs.

OVEN GUIDE: You may find cooking times vary depending on the oven you are using. For convection ovens, as a general rule, set the oven temperature to 35°F (20°C) lower than indicated in the recipe.

We have used 20 ml (4 teaspoon) tablespoon measures. If you are using a 15 ml (3 teaspoon) tablespoon add an extra teaspoon of the ingredient for each tablespoon specified.